ON THE EDGE
IN YOUR DREAMS

Henry Billings
Melissa Billings

McGraw Hill Wright Group

Series Editor: Amy Collins
Executive Editor: Linda Kwil
Production Manager: Genevieve Kelley
Marketing Manager: Sean Klunder
Cover Design: Michael E. Kelly

 **Wright Group**

Send all inquiries to:
Wright Group/McGraw-Hill
130 East Randolph Street, Suite 400
Chicago, Illinois 60601

ISBN: 0-07-285194-5

Printed in the United States of America.

5 6 7 8 9 10 QPD 08

CONTENTS

To the Student

Strange things that cannot be explained happen to people every day. UFO sightings, out-of-body experiences, premonitions, and reports of alien abduction have confounded people for hundreds of years. The stories in *On the Edge: In Your Dreams* go deep into the mysteries of true crime and the paranormal. A man murders his wife while sleepwalking. A woman suffers from amnesia and doesn't remember her own husband. A couple is abducted by aliens as they drive down a highway in Australia. People across Britain have premonitions of a disaster days before an avalanche of coal crashes into a junior school, killing 116 students. These stories may mystify, scare, or shock you. They may seem very hard to believe. Only you can decide if they are true or not.

As you read the stories in this book, you will be developing your reading skills. The lessons will help you increase your reading speed while you improve your reading comprehension, critical thinking skills, and vocabulary. Many of the exercises are similar to what you will see on state and national tests. Learning how to complete them will help you prepare for tests you will take in the future. Some of the exercises encourage you to write sentence or paragraph responses. As you write your opinions, you will learn to support them with specific examples from the stories you read.

You may not believe in out-body-experiences, aliens, or premonitions. You may think hypnosis is a hoax. Amnesia may strike you as too strange to ever really happen. Whether you think the stories are true or not, one thing is for certain: you won't be able to take your eyes off each page until you've read the book cover to cover.

How to Use This Book

ABOUT THE BOOK *On the Edge: In Your Dreams* has ten units, each of which contain two stories and a lesson. The stories are about true crime, the paranormal, and ordinary people who do very bizarre things. Each story is followed by a page of reading comprehension exercises. These exercises will help you to better understand the article. At the end of each unit are exercises that help develop vocabulary and critical thinking skills. These exercises will assist your understanding of the similarities between the two stories and to relate them to your own experiences.

THE SAMPLE LESSON The first lesson in the book is a sample that demonstrates how the units are organized. The sample lesson will show you how to complete the exercises. The correct answers to the questions are included.

WORKING THROUGH EACH UNIT Begin each unit by looking at the photograph. Before you begin reading, think about your reaction to the photo and predict what you think the article might be about. Then read the article.

Sometimes you or your teacher may want to time how long it takes you to read a story. You can write your time in the circle at the end of each story. Use the Words-per-Minute Table on page 120 to find your reading speed and record it on the Plotting Your Progress graph on page 121. As you read through the book, you will be able to watch your reading speed improve on the graph.

After you read the article and record your speed, begin the exercises. The comprehension section will test your understanding of what you have read. The vocabulary exercises will include words that were used in both stories. The critical thinking exercises will help you build analytical skills. Some of the exercises will ask you to write a paragraph giving your thoughts and opinions about the stories. Answers to all the exercises can be found in the *On the Edge Teacher's Guide.*

SAMPLE LESSON

SELECTION 1

Night Wanderers

Edward Amonte was having a nightmare—a really bad nightmare. The nine-year-old boy dreamed that his parents were being killed. As he dreamed, Edward began to move. He got out of bed, walked into the kitchen, and climbed up onto the sink. Still asleep, he opened the window of his family's New York City apartment. Then Edward jumped out onto the street, three stories below.

Edward was badly hurt in the fall. Rescue workers took him to the hospital. He woke up enough to describe his bad dream. But on January 16, 2001, he died from his injuries.

No one is sure what causes sleepwalking. It seems to happen when signals in the brain get mixed up. Sleepwalkers wake up enough to move around. But their conscious minds stay asleep. Sometimes they act out a dream. Other times their actions make no sense at all. Sleepwalkers may start moving furniture. They may get out the lawnmower and mow the lawn. They may drive off in a car or go ride a horse. One teenager hopped on a train. He was almost a hundred miles from home when he woke up.

A TV movie may have caused Reece Klaudt's sleepwalking. Reece was a 21-year-old from Illinois. In 1997, he went on a trip to Florida. There he watched a TV movie about a sinking ship. People were jumping overboard to save themselves. Later that night, Reece walked out onto the balcony of his room. It was six stories off the ground. Still asleep, Reece did what he had seen the people on TV do—he tried to jump off the ship. Because he landed on bushes, he wasn't badly hurt. He walked away with just a few minor injuries.

Roger Goodwin also sleepwalked off a balcony. In 1997, 28-year-old Goodwin was living in Greece. He had an apartment on the fourth floor. One night, Goodwin went onto the balcony and jumped sixty feet to the ground below. An awning slowed his fall. Even so, he landed on a concrete path and broke several bones in his back. Goodwin doesn't know what caused him to jump. He said, "I don't remember a thing—just the sight of people looking over me when I suddenly woke up."

In 1997, a sleepwalker jumped off a boat near the coast of New Zealand. It happened at 5:30 in the morning. The man's friends saw him walk up onto the deck. They could tell he wasn't really awake. Then they heard a splash. It took a helicopter to fish the man out of the water. By then, he was almost dead.

One sleepwalker tried to jump out of a hot-air balloon. David

Hempleman-Adams was flying over the North Pole. It was a long trip. At one point, he fell asleep and began to sleepwalk. Only a safety harness kept him from falling to his death.

David Richards didn't jump *off* anything. Instead, he jumped *on* something. Richards stood up on his bed and began jumping in his sleep. But his ceiling fan was on at the time. The fan hit him and sent him flying across the room.

Sleepwalkers don't always jump; sometimes they fall. One 14-year-old boy sleepwalked during a camping trip. He fell off a cliff. The boy lived. But he broke his nose and knocked out some teeth. Eighteen-year-old David Wright also fell off a cliff. He landed in the Pacific Ocean. He bobbed in the water for eight hours. At last a fisherman heard his call for help and picked him up.

In 1998, 77-year-old James Currens sleepwalked out of his Florida home. He fell down a hill behind his house and rolled into a pond. He woke up and tried to climb out, but he couldn't. He was stuck in mud. To make things worse, his splashing attracted alligators. Eight or ten of them began swimming over to him.

A neighbor had heard James' screams for help and dialed 911. By the time the police came, the alligators were just a few feet from Currens. He was trying to beat them away with his cane. The police pulled him out of the water in time. But it was a close call.

Mark Wilton's sleepwalking caused different problems. Everyone in Charleville, Australia, knew that this 11-year-old boy sleepwalked. He did it so often that his friends called him the "Nightwalker." But Mark didn't just walk

in his sleep. He hid. His parents often found him curled up in a closet or cupboard, sound asleep. So his mother wasn't too worried when she went into his room one morning in the spring of 2001 and found his bed empty. She thought he would be in one of his usual hiding spots.

Mrs. Wilton looked all over the house. But she couldn't find Mark anywhere. She checked every room. She looked in every closet and cupboard. She began to fear that Mark had left the house. She thought he might have fallen into the nearby river.

Mrs. Wilton called the police. They launched a big search. Firefighters and friends joined in. They walked along the banks of the river. There was no sign of the missing boy. Then one officer checked the Wilton home again. He found Mark, safe and sound. The boy was fast asleep under his brother's bed.

When you finish reading, subtract your start time from your end time. This is how long it took you to read the selection. Enter your reading time below.

If you have been timed while reading this article, enter your reading time below. Then turn to the Words-per-Minute Table on page 120 and look up your reading speed (words per minute). Enter your reading speed on the graph on page 121.

Reading Time: Selection 1

_____ : _____
MINUTES   SECONDS

Work through the exercises on this page.
If necessary, refer back to the story.

UNDERSTANDING IDEAS Choose the best answer to check your understanding of the story you just read.

1. **Edward Amonte's injuries were a direct result of**

   A waking up and describing his bad dream

   B dreaming that his parents were being killed

   C *falling out of a window while sleepwalking*

   D getting out of bed and walking into the kitchen

2. **Which picture BEST describes what caused Reece Klaudt's actions while sleepwalking?**

1. a television program

2. train

3. boat

4. hot air balloon

   F *Picture 1*

   G Picture 2

   H Picture 3

   J Picture 4

3. **Mark Wilton would probably not get hurt while sleepwalking because he would simply**

   A walk in circles

   B try to take a shower

   C jump up and down on his bed

   D *hide somewhere in the house*

4. **Based on examples of sleepwalking in the article, the reader can conclude that people who walk in their sleep are**

   F *slightly awake*

   G always injured

   H angry at somebody

   J acting out a bad dream

SUMMARIZE For each blank, choose the word that best completes the meaning of the paragraph to check your understanding of the story.

fall	age	sense
television	dangerous	unconscious

Sleepwalkers can be any _____*age*_____.

Sometimes, sleepwalkers like Reece Klaudt appear

to be acting out something they have seen on

_____*television*_____. Other times, sleepwalkers

do things that don't make any _____*sense*_____

at all. Not all sleepwalkers jump off things; some of them

_____*fall*_____. Sleepwalking is an act

of the _____*unconscious*_____ mind, and it can

be very _____*dangerous*_____.

IF YOU WERE THERE Imagine that you find a member of your family sleepwalking. What would you do? Write a brief paragraph explaining your actions. Be sure to include examples from the story to support your response.

If I found someone sleepwalking, I would first

move him away from anything dangerous. I wouldn't

want him to fall out of a window or off a balcony.

Then I would try to wake him up and find out what

he was thinking.

Read the next article and complete the exercises that follow.

The Sleepwalking Defense

It made no sense. Scott Falater had no reason to kill his wife. Scott and Yarmila had been married for twenty years. By all accounts, they had a happy and loving marriage. They also had two teenage children, a nice house in Phoenix, Arizona, and plenty of money. Yet on January 16, 1997, Scott stabbed Yarmila 44 times. Then he threw her body into their swimming pool and held her head under the water until she stopped breathing.

When the police arrived, Scott claimed he didn't know a thing about the crime. He said he had gone to bed about 9:30 P.M. and didn't remember anything after that. But the police had proof that Scott was the killer. So Scott's lack of memory became his only defense. He was not guilty, his lawyer said, because he had killed his wife while sleepwalking.

At the trial, Scott's neighbor, Greg Koons, told what he had seen. On the night of January 16, Koons went to bed early. But he woke up sometime after 10 P.M. He heard screams coming from the Falaters' yard. When he went outside and peered over the fence, he saw Yarmila lying by the pool. The Falaters' pool lights were on. So Koons had a clear view of Scott walking into the house. Soon Scott came back out wearing a pair of gloves. As Koons watched, Scott dragged Yarmila's body into the pool. He pushed his wife's head under the water.

Only then did Koons realize what was happening. He ran inside and dialed 911. He told the police he had just seen a murder.

When police got to the Falaters' home, they saw Yarmila's body floating in the pool. She had been stabbed, then drowned. Scott was inside. He seemed to have no idea why the police were there. They took him to the police station and questioned him. Still, he didn't seem to know what was going on. When detective John Norman told him Yarmila was dead, Scott began to cry.

"I want to know why you did it," Norman said.

"I'm sorry. I don't remember doing it," Scott told him.

Norman asked more questions, but Scott stuck to his story.

"What did you guys argue over, Scott?" Norman asked.

"Nothing," Scott insisted. "Nothing. How did she die?"

Scott didn't seem to know that he had blood on his neck. He didn't know he had a fresh cut on his finger. He was shocked when Norman told him what Greg Koons had seen.

Scott hired a lawyer named Mike Kimerer. As Kimerer got ready for the trial, he learned that Scott had often sleepwalked as a child. Kimerer did some research. He became convinced that Scott had been sleepwalking when he killed Yarmila.

Experts say that sleepwalking is often triggered by stress. Indeed, Scott was under great pressure at work. He was an engineer at a big company. But things were not going well in his department.

Kimerer brought in an expert to study Scott's brain waves and muscle actions during sleep. These fit the pattern for sleepwalkers. Also, Scott had a history of getting violent if his sleepwalking was interrupted. His sister once tried to stop Scott from walking out of the house in his sleep. "He kind of lifted me up and tossed me," she said. "His face looked almost demonic when he reacted to me."

Sleepwalking would explain why Scott did so many strange things the night of the murder. After all, he kept the pool lights on while he killed Yarmila. He put gloves on *after* he stabbed her. And he left her body lying in the pool in plain view.

Most of all, sleepwalking would explain why Scott killed Yarmila. He had no motive. He and Yarmila really did seem to be happily married.

Prosecutors laughed at the sleepwalking theory. They pointed out that Scott hid the murder weapon, along with his own bloody clothes, in the garage. That was not the random act of a sleepwalker. They also pointed out that most sleepwalking episodes last five to ten minutes. Scott's supposedly lasted an hour. And they pointed out that Scott normally took out his contact lenses when he went to bed. On January 16, though, he left them in. That way he could see what he was doing when he killed Yarmila.

Scott Falater was not the first person to use the sleepwalking defense. More than twenty other people have used it. Steven Steinberg said he was sleeping when he stabbed and killed his wife in 1982. The jury believed him. They found Steinberg not guilty. In Canada, a jury believed Ken Parks, too. Parks had killed his mother-in-law with a tire iron in 1992.

But this time, the sleepwalking defense didn't work. Scott's trial lasted almost a month. But the jury took just eight hours to reach a decision. They found Scott Falater guilty of murder.

Falater was not surprised. He knew his story was hard to believe. But, he said, it was the truth. "I'm not this monster that they're trying to paint me to be," he said. "I know who I am on the inside. . . . I am innocent."

If you have been timed while reading this article, enter your reading time below. Then turn to the Words-per-Minute Table on page 120 and look up your reading speed (words per minute). Enter your reading speed on the graph on page 121.

Reading Time: Selection 2

_____ : _____
MINUTES   SECONDS

UNDERSTANDING IDEAS Circle the letter of the best answer.

1. **Which statement belongs in the empty box?**

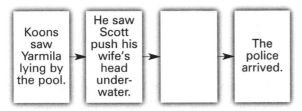

Koons saw Yarmila lying by the pool. → He saw Scott push his wife's head underwater. → ☐ → The police arrived.

   A He woke up sometime after 10 P.M.

   B He saw Scott stab Yarmila 44 times.

   C He heard Scott and Yarmila having an argument.

   D He dialed 911 and told police he had just seen a murder.

2. **Which statement best summarizes Scott's defense?**

   F He was not home when his wife was killed.

   G His wife was sleepwalking and fell into the pool.

   H He was sleepwalking and didn't remember killing her.

   J His wife had enemies who were more likely to kill her.

3. **Which is the most convincing evidence that Scott might have been sleepwalking?**

   A He had no motive.

   B He had told a neighbor he wished Yarmila was dead.

   C He and Yarmila fought a lot.

   D He had a history of being violent.

4. **The jury probably found Scott Falater guilty because he**

   F hid the murder weapon

   G hid his bloody clothes in the garage

   H wore his contact lenses when he went to bed

   J did all of the above

SUMMARIZE For each blank, choose the word that best completes the meaning of the paragraph.

defense	murdered	floating
cry	convicted	sleepwalking

On January 16, 1997, Scott Falater

_____ his wife. Police found

her body _____ in the pool.

When Scott was told his wife was dead, he began to

_____. Scott's lawyer said that Scott

had been _____ when he killed his

wife. But he was still _____ of

murder by a jury. More than twenty other people have

also used the sleepwalking _____.

IF YOU WERE THERE Write a brief paragraph explaining what you would do if you were one of Scott and Yarmila Falaters' teenage children. Whom would you believe? Be sure to include examples from the story to support your response.

_____

_____

_____

_____

_____

_____

_____

_____

USE CONTEXT CLUES When you read, you may find a word whose meaning is unfamiliar to you. When that happens, you can look up the word's meaning in the dictionary. You can also find out what the word means by looking for context clues. These are words or sentences that come before or after the word. Context clues can be words with the same or opposite meanings as the unfamiliar word. They may also be an example or definition of the unfamiliar word.

Read each excerpt from the stories you just read. Circle the letter with the best meaning of the underlined word.

1. **Sleepwalkers wake up enough to move around. But their <u>conscious</u> minds stay asleep.**

   A the part of the brain that is aware

   B the evil part of the brain

   C the part of the brain that controls the muscles

   D the part of the brain that controls emotions

2. **Later that night, Reece walked out onto the <u>balcony</u> of his room. It was six stories off the ground.**

   F the sitting area

   G the carpeted area of the room

   H a platform enclosed by a railing

   J the deck on a ship

3. **He [Greg Koons] heard screams coming from the Falaters' yard. When he went outside and <u>peered</u> over the fence, he saw Yarmila lying by the pool.**

   A jumped

   B yelled

   C climbed

   D looked

4. **Experts say that sleepwalking is often <u>triggered</u> by stress. Indeed, Scott was under great pressure at work.**

   F halted

   G set off

   H dreamed

   J responsible for

5. **<u>Prosecutors</u> laughed at the sleepwalking theory. They pointed out that Scott hid the murder weapon, along with his own bloody clothes, in the garage.**

   A trial lawyers

   B Yarmila's family

   C police

   D doctors

PUT WORDS INTO CONTEXT Complete the paragraph using the underlined words from the exercise on this page.

Scott Falater claimed he was not

_____ of what he was doing.

He said his sleepwalking had been

_____ by pressure at work. When

the witness _____ into the

neighbor's yard, he saw a murderer, not a sleepwalker.

The _____ in the case against

Scott Falater did not believe his story.

ANTONYMS An antonym is a word that has the opposite meaning of another word. For example, *remember* is an antonym for the word *forget*.

Circle the letter of the word or phrase that means the OPPOSITE of the underlined word.

1. **Edward Amonte was having a <u>nightmare</u>—a really bad nightmare.**
   A scary dream
   B good dream
   C bad dream
   D weird dream

2. **He walked away with just a few <u>minor</u> injuries.**
   F small
   G unimportant
   H deep
   J big

3. **He <u>bobbed</u> in the water for eight hours.**
   A sank
   B swam
   C floated
   D twirled

4. **She thought he would be in one of his <u>usual</u> hiding spots.**
   F different
   G normal
   H typical
   J outdoor

5. **So Scott's <u>lack</u> of memory became his only defense.**
   A abundance of
   B small amount of
   C missing
   D perfect

ANTONYM ANALOGIES Analogies show similar patterns between words. Antonym analogies show patterns between words that have opposite meanings. For example, *large* is to *small* as *tall* is to *short*. For each blank, choose an underlined word from the exercise on this page to correctly complete the analogy.

1. *Minimum* is to *maximum* as

_____ is to *major*.

2. *Real* is to *make-believe* as

_____ is to *pleasant dream*.

3. *Simple* is to *elegant* as

_____ is to *extraordinary*

4. *Poverty* is to *riches* as

_____ is to *excess*.

5. *Floated* is to *sank* as

_____ is to *went down*.

ORGANIZE IDEAS The main ideas in a story are the larger, more general topics that are covered. The specific details are the facts that clarify or support the main ideas. Fill in the chart by using the items listed at the right. If the bulleted item is a main idea from the story, write it in the row marked "Main Idea." If the item is a detail that supports the main idea, write it in a row marked "Detail."

"Night Wanderers"
Main Idea:
Detail:
Detail:
Detail:
Detail:

"The Sleepwalking Defense"
Main Idea:
Detail:
Detail:
Detail:
Detail:

- Sleepwalkers wake up enough to move around. But their conscious minds stay asleep.

- He kept the pool lights on while he killed Yarmila.

- As he dreamed, Edward opened the window and jumped out.

- He didn't seem to know what was going on when police questioned him.

- One teenager hopped on a train and was almost a hundred miles from home when he woke up.

- He left the body in the pool in plain view.

- Goodwin doesn't know why he jumped from the balcony of his fourth floor apartment.

- Sleepwalking would explain why Scott did so many strange things the night of the murder.

- Still asleep, Reece did what he had seen people on TV do—he tried to jump off the ship.

- He put gloves on *after* he stabbed her.

SUPPORT THE MAIN IDEA Write a paragraph about sleepwalking. State the main idea in the first sentence. Then use details from both stories to support your main idea.

_____

_____

_____

_____

_____

_____

_____

_____

DRAW CONCLUSIONS A conclusion is a judgment based on information. The way you draw a conclusion is to think about what you've read and see if you can make a judgment, or general statement, about it. Read this paragraph about sleepwalking. Then choose the best answer to each question.

[1] Sleepwalking can cause people to do strange things unconsciously. [2] It is not uncommon for people to harm themselves when sleepwalking. [3] Sleepwalkers have jumped out of windows, fallen off cliffs, and walked off balconies. [4] Some sleepwalkers imitate things they have seen on TV. [5] Other sleepwalkers act out their dreams.

1. **Which conclusion you can draw based on the paragraph above?**

    A Sleepwalkers often pretend to be asleep.

    B Sleepwalkers are not aware of their actions.

    C Sleepwalkers usually don't leave the house.

    D Sleepwalkers are always acting out dreams.

2. **Which sentence from the paragraph explains how sleepwalking can be dangerous?**

    F Sentence 1

    G Sentence 3

    H Sentence 4

    J Sentence 5

3. **Which sentence from the paragraph helps you conclude that dreams and sleepwalking are related?**

    A Sentence 2

    B Sentence 3

    C Sentence 4

    D Sentence 5

JUDGE THE EVIDENCE When you make a conclusion, you must judge if the information presented is accurate or convincing. Choose the best answer.

1. **Which statement best supports the conclusion that sleepwalking can be used as a defense for murder?**

    A Prosecutors laughed at the sleepwalking theory.

    B Scott Falater knew that his story was hard to believe.

    C As Kimerer got ready for the trial, he learned that Scott had often sleepwalked as a child.

    D A jury believed Steven Steinberg, who said he was asleep when he killed his wife.

2. **Which statement best supports the conclusion that the body of a sleepwalker is awake?**

    F Sleepwalkers wake up enough to move around.

    G Sleepwalkers vaguely remember what they have done.

    H Sleepwalkers are often under great pressure at work.

    J Sleepwalkers have similar brain waves and muscle actions.

YOUR OWN CONCLUSION Pretend that you are part of a jury that must decide whether Scott Falater was guilty or not. State your conclusion and support it with examples from both stories.

_____

_____

_____

_____

_____

_____

Good-bye, Sweet World

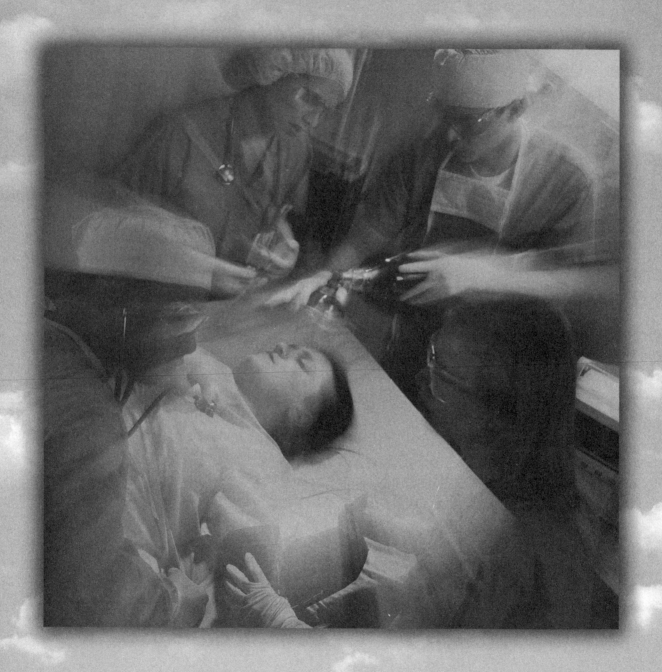

When the 44-year-old man was brought to the hospital, he was close to death. In fact, by most measures, he *was* dead. He was unconscious. His heart was not beating. His brain showed no activity at all.

Doctors worked hard to get his heart pumping again. They put him on a machine that breathed air into his lungs. When a nurse had to put a tube down his throat, she noticed the man's false teeth and took them out. At last, the medical team saw some signs of life. They moved him to the intensive care unit and hoped for the best.

A week later, the man was not only alive, he was awake and talking. That didn't surprise the staff. What did surprise them was that he remembered the nurse who took out his false teeth. He remembered other details as well. How was this possible? He had been lifeless at the time. The man's explanation startled them. He had watched the whole scene from outside his body.

The man had had a near-death experience, or NDE. As death approached, he had felt himself rise out of his body. He was able to look down at the doctors. He watched them trying to save his life.

Many people report having NDEs. These experiences can take many forms.

Often people seem to float above their own bodies. They feel very peaceful. Some say they are drawn toward a bright light. They may hear a loud noise. Loved ones who are already dead may be beckoning them. Yet they can look down and see their physical forms in the room below. They can hear doctors and nurses trying to bring them back to life. Often they are torn between their desire to move toward the light and their desire to return to their bodies.

Doctors used to scoff at the idea of near-death experiences. Some still do. They say no one can really leave his or her body. It can all be explained by science. The dying brain sends out chemicals that produce a feeling of calm. Thoughts and memories become scrambled, producing images of dead loved ones. The light and the noise are just the last gasps of a brain trying to function without blood or oxygen.

That still leaves the false teeth. How could a person with no brain activity know who took out his false teeth? Some doctors suggest that certain pathways to the brain may stay open even as death approaches. The eyes and ears may still be sending messages to the brain. So if the person is resuscitated, those messages get through.

Regardless of what causes NDEs, the fact remains that they can have a huge effect on people. Many people feel as though they have met God—or at least have connected with the world beyond death. That, in turn, changes their lives. If you don't believe that, just ask Pam Barrett. For years, Barrett was a big force in Canadian politics. She was a leader of Canada's New Democratic Party. But on February 1, 2000, Pam Barrett had a near-death experience. It was an experience she would never forget.

Pam felt fine when the day began. She went to have some dental work done by her friend, dentist David Oyen. He gave her a shot of anesthesia in her mouth. But something went wrong. Pam had an allergic reaction to the shot. "My entire body went numb," she later recalled. "My throat swelled up so much I couldn't breathe."

Pam sat up straight in the dentist's chair. "David, I'm dying," she cried. Then she fell back into the chair. A few moments later, she sat up again. "I'm going," she said.

At that point, Pam stopped breathing. She suddenly felt "warm and peaceful." It was "like being wrapped in a warm, charcoal blanket." She could feel herself hovering between life and death. The next thing she knew, she was back in the dentist's chair.

David performed mouth-to-mouth resuscitation on her. When rescue workers arrived, they rushed her to a nearby hospital. There, Pam again felt herself moving toward death. As a staff worker talked to her, Pam floated toward the ceiling. She found herself looking down at the staff worker. She was also looking down at her own lifeless body lying on the bed.

Pam soon floated back into her body. But the out-of-body experience had changed her forever.

"When I recovered from that episode, I was a different person," she said. "What this does to you spiritually is indescribable." For one thing, Barrett lost her fear of death. Beyond that, she felt God had sent her a message—and she knew it was important. She couldn't really put it into words. But the very next day, Pam took drastic action. She announced that she was quitting her job and walking away from politics.

"My decision to do this is extremely spiritual," she told reporters. "I need a new path. I need to do something and I can't tell you what it is and I cannot explain the spiritual connection."

Other people have been similarly affected by near-death experiences. Some describe themselves as more loving or more peaceful after their brush with death. Many say their fears have evaporated. And some have set new goals for themselves. So even if NDEs really are just an illusion, they have changed the lives of thousands of people.

If you have been timed while reading this article, enter your reading time below. Then turn to the Words-per-Minute Table on page 120 and look up your reading speed (words per minute). Enter your reading speed on the graph on page 121.

Reading Time: Selection 1

_____ : _____
MINUTES   SECONDS

14

UNDERSTANDING IDEAS Circle the letter of the best answer.

1. **Which statement belongs in the empty box?**

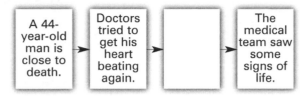

   A The man was brought to the hospital.

   B A nurse removed his false teeth.

   C The staff brought him to the intensive care unit.

   D The man was awake and talking a week later.

2. **Why was the staff surprised when the man remembered who took his false teeth?**

   F He had a near-death experience.

   G He seemed to float above his body.

   H He had no brain activity at the time.

   J He was watching them trying to save his life.

3. **What was the cause of Pam Barrett's near-death experience?**

   A She had an allergic reaction to anesthesia.

   B She wanted to walk away from politics.

   C She cannot explain the spiritual connection.

   D She felt herself hovering between life and death.

4. **Based on examples of near-death experiences in the story, the reader can conclude that the episodes are**

   F warm and peaceful

   G spiritual, but very real

   H based on scientific knowledge

   J different from person to person

SUMMARIZE For each blank, choose the word that best completes the meaning of the paragraph.

body	experiences	
breathing	lives	watched

There are many examples of near-death

_____. A man who had been lifeless

later said he had _____ the doctors

try to save his life. Pam Barrett had stopped

_____ while at the dentist's. At the

hospital, she found herself looking down at her own

_____ lying on the bed.

These out-of-body episodes have changed the

_____ of those who have

experienced them.

IF YOU WERE THERE What do you think you would do if you had a near-death experience? Write a brief paragraph explaining your actions. Be sure to include examples from the story to support your response.

_____

_____

_____

_____

_____

_____

Travels to Another World

"In the spring of 1958 I was living a reasonably normal life with a reasonably normal family." That's how Robert Monroe put it in his book *Journeys Out of the Body*. But as Monroe noted, his "normal" life was about to change. He was about to take some trips that were truly out of this world.

Monroe, a successful businessman, was lying on the couch one Sunday afternoon when he suddenly started to shake. The shaking stopped when he sat up. But over the next few weeks, he had more of these episodes. They came when he was lying down resting. Monroe thought he might have a brain tumor or other disease. But doctors found nothing wrong with him.

Then Monroe discovered that he could move his arm during these spells. He pushed his fingers against the rug on the floor. To his surprise, he pushed his fingers *through* the rug. He touched the wood underneath. He felt a nail and some sawdust. He dipped his fingers into a pool of water.

"I was wide awake," he wrote. "I could feel myself lying on the bed, the covers over my body, the pillow under my head, my chest rising and falling as I breathed . . . yet, impossibly, my hand was playing in a pool of water, and my arm felt as if it was stuck down through the floor."

Soon things got even more bizarre. During the next spell, Monroe happened to think about flying. All at once he found himself up in the air. "I was floating against the ceiling, bouncing gently with any movement I made." When he looked down, he saw his body still lying on the bed. That was when Monroe knew what had happened. He had stumbled upon a form of "astral projection." In other words, he had found a way to travel outside his body.

Monroe came to believe that each person has two bodies. One is our regular physical shell. The other is what Monroe called the Second Body. This one is not physical. And it doesn't always stay put. In fact, Monroe believed that most people leave their bodies during sleep. This would explain why dreams seem so strange—and yet so real. Dreams would be the experiences we have when we are floating around without our bodies.

Monroe didn't invent the idea of astral projection. It has been around for centuries. People in ancient Egypt believed in it. So did people in ancient India and China. Most of the world's religions are based on the notion that people have some sort of spirit that can live on after the body dies.

Monroe began taking trips in his Second Body. He thought others could learn to do the same. The first step, he said, was to get rid of fear. A person has to relax. He or she must drift into a state that is on the "edge of sleep." That's when the shaking begins. After the Second Body gets free from the physical self, it can travel to any number of places.

Monroe set up tests to prove that this travel was taking place. He tried to visit a friend's new home in his Second Body. He hoped he would be able to describe what the house looked like. He tried to read a five-digit number written on a card in the next room. It turned out that he couldn't do these things. He had trouble getting his Second Body to go where he wanted. Sometimes it took him to a strange new place. This place looked like an odd version of the "normal" world. There were cars on the streets, but the cars had no motors. There were houses, but the houses had no lights. Monroe called this place "Locale III."

Other times Monroe's Second Body took him to "Locale II." This was where he said people went in their dreams. It was not at all like the "normal" world. For one thing, there was no concept of time. The air swirled with fears and desires. It was impossible to know what would happen next. Sometimes Monroe enjoyed himself. Other times he did not.

Skeptics, of course, thought all this was absurd. They didn't think human consciousness could exist apart from the body. They figured that some of Monroe's "travels" were ordinary dreams. The rest were the results of wishful thinking.

Robert Monroe knew what skeptics were saying. But he didn't care. He went ahead with his work. He set up a research team to study his ideas. This team coined the phrase "out-of-body experience." In 1974, Monroe set up the Monroe Institute. It offered classes to the public. These classes were designed to help people gain better access to their Second Bodies.

Robert Monroe died in 1995. But his daughter Laurie picked up where he left off. So today Monroe's work goes on. Many people are interested in the ideas he put forward. They believe they have Second Bodies. They believe they can travel to places beyond the "normal" world. They remember well what Monroe once said: "The greatest illusion is that man has limitations."

If you have been timed while reading this article, enter your reading time below. Then turn to the Words-per-Minute Table on page 120 and look up your reading speed (words per minute). Enter your reading speed on the graph on page 121.

Reading Time: Selection 2

_____ : _____
MINUTES   SECONDS

UNDERSTANDING IDEAS Circle the letter of the best answer.

1. **Why did Robert Monroe think that he might have a brain tumor or other disease?**

   A His vision went blurry.

   B He started having terrible headaches.

   C He started shaking for no reason.

   D He found an unusual lump on his skull.

2. **What did Monroe say he discovered during one of his spells?**

   F He could move his arm.

   G He had trouble breathing.

   H He realized he was sleeping.

   J He could get up and walk around.

3. **Monroe believed that most people**

   A don't have Second Bodies

   B leave their physical bodies during sleep

   C are too stressed to have an out-of-body experience

   D can control what happens to their Second Bodies

4. **Many people are interested in Monroe's ideas probably because they believe that**

   F Monroe's travels were ordinary dreams

   G travels outside the body would be dangerous

   H some sort of spirit exists beyond the physical body

   J human consciousness could not exist outside the body

5. **If a person wants to gain better access to a Second Body, he or she would most likely go to**

   A Locale II in a dream

   B the Monroe Institute

   C Laurie Monroe's research library

   D places beyond the "normal" world

SUMMARIZE For each blank, choose the word that best completes the meaning of the paragraph.

classes	flying	normal	Second Body
travel	float	trips	

Robert Monroe was living a _____

life. Then he found that he could

_____ outside his body during

certain times. Once he said he was able to

_____ near the ceiling while thinking

about _____ _____. Monroe started to take

_____ in his _____.

In 1974, Monroe set up the Monroe Institute to offer

_____ to people who wanted to learn

more about their Second Bodies.

IF YOU WERE THERE Write a brief paragraph explaining whether or not you would go to the Monroe Institute to learn more about the possibility of a Second Body. Be sure to include examples from the story to support your response.

_____

_____

_____

_____

_____

USE CONTEXT CLUES When you read, you may find a word whose meaning is unfamiliar to you. When that happens, you can look up the word's meaning in the dictionary. You can also find out what the word means by looking for context clues. These are words or sentences that come before or after the word. Context clues can be words with the same or opposite meanings as the unfamiliar word. They may also be an example or definition of the unfamiliar word.

Read each excerpt from the stories you just read. Circle the letter with the best meaning of the underlined word.

1. **He had been lifeless at the time. The man's explanation startled them. He had watched the whole scene from outside his body.**

   A saddened

   B interested

   C surprised

   D amused

2. **Doctors used to scoff at the idea of near-death experiences. Some still do. They say no one can really leave his or her body.**

   F mock

   G embrace

   H get angry

   J like

3. **Pam took drastic action. She announced that she was quitting her job and walking away from politics.**

   A prime

   B extreme

   C moderate

   D positive

4. **Soon things got even more bizarre. During the next spell, Monroe happened to think about flying.**

   F odd

   G usual

   H dark

   J funny

5. **Skeptics, of course, thought all this was absurd. They didn't think human consciousness could exist apart from the body.**

   A believers

   B doctors

   C teachers

   D doubters

PUT WORDS INTO CONTEXT Complete the paragraph using the underlined words from the exercise on this page.

Do you consider yourself a _____,

or do you believe that _____ things

like out-of-body experiences can happen? Would you be

_____ if you heard someone

talk about having two bodies? Monroe would likely have

said that if you _____ at the idea

of traveling outside your body, it probably won't happen

to you.

SYNONYMS A synonym is a word that has the same, or nearly the same, meaning as another word. For example, *happy* and *glad* are synonyms.

Circle the letter of the word that has almost the SAME meaning as the underlined word.

1. **As death underlined{approached}, he felt himself rise out of his body.**
   A overtook
   B exited
   C came near
   D surprised

2. **Loved ones who are already dead may be beckoning them.**
   F signaling
   G scaring
   H confusing
   J warning

3. **Thoughts and memories become scrambled, producing images of dead loved ones.**
   A forgotten
   B cooked
   C mixed up
   D hard to see

4. **But over the next few weeks, he had more of these episodes.**
   F TV shows
   G incidents
   H games
   J sodas

5. **Skeptics, of course, thought all this was absurd.**
   A backward
   B understandable
   C poor
   D ridiculous

ANALOGIES As you have seen in previous exercises, analogies show relationships and patterns between words. The relationships can be very different things, not just synonyms and antonyms. For example, *hat* is to *head* as *glove* is to *hand*. The first words (*hat* and *glove*) are meant to cover the second words (*head* and *hand*). For each blank, choose an underlined word from the exercise on this page to correctly complete the analogy. You will only use one of the underlined words.

1. *Stirred* is to *coffee* as

   _____ is to *eggs*.

2. *Sad* is to *unhappy* as

   _____ is to *foolish*.

3. *Agreeing* is to *nodding* as

   _____ is to *waving*.

4. *Reached* is to *get* as

   _____ is to *meet*.

5. *Words* are to a *sentence* as

   _____ are to a *story*.

ORGANIZE THE FACTS A summary retells the major points of a story. Minor details and examples are not included. To write a summary, first you must decide what the most important points are. You can do this by making a list. Then write a paragraph using the main points from your list. The paragraph is your summary.

Look at the major points listed under "Good-bye, Sweet World." Fill in the missing information for number 5. Then list the major points of "Travels to Another World."

"Good-bye, Sweet World"
1. Many people have NDEs, or near-death experiences, that can take many forms.
2. Some experiences can be explained by science, but some cannot.
3. One 44-year-old man was almost dead, but he remembered the nurse who removed his false teeth.
4. Pam Barrett felt herself floating on the ceiling and looking at her own lifeless body.
5.

"Travels to Another World"
1. Robert Monroe discovered a way to travel outside his body.
2.
3.
4.
5.

SUMMARIZE THE MAJOR POINTS Using the major points listed above, write a brief paragraph summarizing "Travels to Another World."

_____

_____

_____

_____

_____

_____

_____

_____

_____

_____

MAKE INFERENCES An author doesn't always state an idea directly in a passage, but you can determine what it is by applying your own knowledge and experiences. You can also examine the evidence presented in the text. This is called making an inference. Circle the letter of the best answer.

1. **What can the reader infer from the following sentences?**

    > Doctors used to scoff at the idea of near-death experiences. Some still do.

    A Doctors accept that all NDEs are real.

    B Some doctors now believe people can have NDEs.

    C Doctors will never embrace the idea of NDEs.

    D All doctors who used to mock NDEs now believe in them.

2. **What can the reader infer from Robert Monroe's statement at the beginning of the story?**

    > "In the spring of 1958 I was living a reasonably normal life with a reasonably normal family."

    F Monroe gets fired from his job.

    G Monroe's family will leave him.

    H Something doesn't stay normal for Monroe.

    J Nothing out of the ordinary will happen to Monroe.

3. **Which is the best inference a reader can make about this sentence?**

    > Many people are interested in the ideas that he put forward.

    A Many other people still aren't interested at all.

    B What Monroe says is the truth.

    C The author believes that the doctors are wrong.

    D Everyone should be interested in what Monroe says.

APPLY WHAT YOU KNOW

1. **What do you think the author intended to do in the first paragraph of "Good-bye, Sweet World"?**

    A Make the reader curious.

    B Compare different events.

    C Write an exciting news report.

    D Explain how a hospital works.

2. **By saying "Monroe didn't invent the idea of astral projection" the author probably wanted to**

    F present Monroe as a crazy character

    G make Monroe's story sound more believable

    H convince the reader that Monroe has two bodies

    J inform readers that Monroe is an imaginative guy

JUDGE THE EVIDENCE Based on what you have read from both stories, do you think people are dreaming or actually having these experiences? Write a brief paragraph saying whether or not you believe that people have NDEs. Support your opinion with evidence from the stories you have read.

_____

_____

_____

_____

_____

_____

_____

Married to a Stranger

They first met over the phone. When Kim Carpenter called a sportswear company to buy some baseball jackets, Krickitt Pappas took his order. But this call turned out to be much more than a sales order. Kim and Krickitt liked talking with each other. They just kept chatting. Soon they discovered that they shared many interests. Many more phone calls followed. Kim lived in New Mexico and Krickitt lived in California. For six months they talked on the phone without ever seeing each other.

At last, in April of 1993, they agreed to meet in person. Krickitt flew to New Mexico. Kim remembered the moment he first saw her. "She got off the plane— I'll never forget," he said. "It was like I'd always known her."

After that, they got together nearly every weekend. In June, Kim surprised Krickitt by showing up at her apartment without warning. With flowers and a ring, he asked Krickitt to be his wife. They were married that fall. For two months Kim and Krickitt lived together as happy newlyweds. Then, in an instant, a car accident changed their lives forever.

It happened on November 24, 1993, when they were headed to visit Krickitt's parents in Phoenix, Arizona. Krickitt was driving and Kim was resting in the back seat. Suddenly, Krickitt swerved to avoid a slow-moving truck. She didn't turn fast enough and hit the back of the truck. A second truck smashed into them from behind. The Carpenters' car flipped over one and a half times. It slid over 100 feet on its roof.

Kim was badly injured. He had a broken hand, a punctured lung, and a bruised heart. But he was in good condition compared to Krickitt. The collapsed roof of the car had crushed her head, fracturing her skull. "I screamed and screamed and screamed for Krickitt and got no answer," said Kim.

Krickitt hung upside down in the car for half an hour waiting for help. When rescuers finally arrived, it took them forty minutes to cut her loose. They rushed her to the hospital, but her condition was grim. Kim thought his wife was going to die. He refused to leave her side to have his own injuries treated.

Krickitt didn't die, but she spent five days in a coma. Slowly the swelling in her brain went down. Her dangerously low blood pressure began to rise. When she came out of her coma, doctors took her off life support. The danger was over. Krickitt was going to live.

But what kind of life would she have? Three weeks after the accident, a nurse asked her what year it was. "1969," Krickitt answered. The nurse asked what her husband's name was. "I'm not married," said Krickitt. When told that she was indeed married, Krickitt named an old boyfriend, Todd, as her husband.

Krickitt had amnesia. The blow to her brain had wiped out all her recent memories. She couldn't remember anything about the last 18 months. She couldn't remember the phone calls with Kim. She couldn't remember the weekend visits. Krickitt still had her older memories, so she knew her parents' names. But she couldn't recall anything at all about her life with Kim. When Kim learned this, he was crushed. He was especially hurt to hear that Krickitt thought she was married to Todd. "I was devastated," he said.

What kind of a marriage would Kim and Krickitt have now? She didn't love him—she didn't even remember him. She felt like she was living with a total stranger. As for Kim, he found that Krickitt's personality had changed. The head injuries left her more outgoing but also more temperamental. She often got angry. She laughed and cried more than the old Krickitt had. In these new circumstances, there was a good chance that Krickitt and Kim might actually grow to hate each other. Adding to the stress was the fact that they had huge medical bills to pay.

"I honestly didn't think our marriage would work," said Kim. But he remembered something. "I made a vow before God—until death do us part." He stayed with Krickitt.

Then one day they got some great advice. A counselor told them to start dating again. He said they had to build a new set of memories. So, like a couple who had just met, Kim and Krickitt went out for pizza. They went shopping and bowling and to the movies. "I got to know my husband again," said Krickitt. "We had fun. And how can you not care deeply for somebody who's stood by you?"

The dating worked. Slowly, Krickitt and Kim fell in love all over again. In 1996, they got married for a second time. Amnesia still prevented Krickitt from remembering her first marriage ceremony. So this second wedding was a brand new experience for her. As she said, "It [was] like the first wedding because I don't have any memory of marrying him."

If you have been timed while reading this article, enter your reading time below. Then turn to the Words-per-Minute Table on page 120 and look up your reading speed (words per minute). Enter your reading speed on the graph on page 121.

Reading Time: Selection 1

_____ : _____
MINUTES   SECONDS

UNDERSTANDING IDEAS Circle the letter of the best answer.

1. Which statement belongs in the empty box?

Kim and Krickitt met by phone. → ☐ → They had a car accident. → Krickitt forgot about Kim.

A They got married.

B They were injured.

C Krickitt was in a coma.

D Kim stayed with Krickitt.

2. Which of the following is a direct and immediate result of the accident?

F Krickitt had amnesia.

G Kim stayed with Krickitt.

H Kim and Krickitt got married a second time.

J Kim and Krickitt avoided a slow-moving truck.

3. Which statement about Krickitt's amnesia is correct?

A She could not recall anything at all.

B Her personality remained the same.

C Her recent memory had been wiped out.

D She could not remember her own parents.

4. If Kim and Krickett did not start dating again, they would most likely

F fall in love again

G end their marriage

H get advice from a counselor

J build a new set of memories

5. Why did Krickitt think that their second wedding was like their first?

A The wedding was a brand new experience for her.

B It was exactly as she remembered the first wedding.

C She does not have any memory of both weddings.

D Just like the first time, she and Kim were in love.

SUMMARIZE For each blank, choose the word that best completes the meaning of the paragraph.

love	survive	
		remember
accident	amnesia	

Kim and Krickitt had been married two months when

a car _____ changed their lives.

Krickitt's injuries caused _____.

She could not _____ her husband.

Kim was not sure that their marriage would

_____. By dating again, they fell in

_____ a second time and remarried.

IF YOU WERE THERE What would you do if someone close to you forgets who you are? Write a brief paragraph explaining your actions. Be sure to include examples from the story to support your response.

_____

_____

_____

_____

_____

_____

_____

_____

The Mystery of Jody Roberts

The mystery began on May 20, 1985. That was the day Jody Roberts failed to show up for work. Her friends at the *News Tribune* in Tacoma, Washington, were surprised.

"It wasn't like her," said editor Rob Tucker.

Days went by. No one saw Jody. Her parents didn't know where she was. Neither did her sisters, brothers, or friends. It was as though the 26-year-old reporter had vanished into thin air.

Meanwhile, 1,300 miles away, another mystery was unfolding. Five days after Jody Roberts disappeared, a woman turned up at a Colorado shopping mall. This woman was dazed and confused. She had no idea who she was. She couldn't remember how she got to the mall. Her pockets contained no identification. All she had was a car key. The key belonged to a Toyota. But it didn't match any car in the parking lot.

Doctors said the woman had amnesia. They believed she had suffered some terrible shock to her system. In response, her brain had wiped out all memories.

No one knew it at the time, but the dazed woman was Jody Roberts. Police in Colorado tried to find out who she was. They ran ads in newspapers and on TV. But no one recognized her. And no one linked her to the missing reporter in Washington state.

Doctors gave the woman a new name: Jane Dee. They gave her a birthday based on how old she looked. For four months she stayed at the Colorado Mental Health Institute. Her memory did not return. So at last she struck out on her own. She already had a college degree, but she didn't know it. So she signed up for classes at the University of Denver. To earn money, she worked as a waitress. In 1989, she moved to Alaska. People in Colorado lost touch with her.

Back in Washington, police were still trying to find out what had happened to Jody Roberts. For a long time, they listed her as a missing person. Finally, in 1997, the police decided Jody had been killed. That made it a murder case. Jody's picture was shown on a Washington news show. A viewer named Madelyn Wright recognized it. Madelyn had waitressed with Jane Dee at a restaurant in Alaska. She called police and told them that Jody Roberts was Jane Dee.

By this time, Jody—known as Jane—was living in the small town of Sitka, Alaska. She was married to a fisherman and had two sets of twin daughters. When police found her, she told them she had no knowledge of her life before 1985. She said her first memory was of standing at the Colorado mall holding a car key. The Roberts family accepted this. They were happy just to know Jody was alive and well.

Others, however, were not so sure. Could Jody Roberts really have forgotten 26 years of her life? Or was she faking amnesia to leave behind a past she didn't want?

Some friends said Jody had been under great stress just before she disappeared. She was drinking a lot. She seemed unhappy. "She wasn't taking care of herself and she was in a foul mood," said friend Mike Bainter. "I could sense that something was wrong."

Others pointed out that Jody closed her bank account just before she disappeared. She took her cats to an animal shelter. Was she planning to go away? Or was something else going on? Maybe she was working on a story that made her fear for her life. Maybe someone was blackmailing her. Or maybe she was in some other kind of trouble.

Neal J. Cohen studies amnesia at the University of Illinois. He said it would be "very unusual" for someone to have memory loss that lasted 12 years. Still, he said it could happen.

As for Jody Roberts, she insisted she was telling the truth. She didn't want to talk to reporters. At last, though, she appeared on a show called *American Journal*. "Amnesia is a funny thing," she said. "I know math but not my name. History but not my past." Roberts said she could list all 50 states. She could remember songs from the 1960s. "But I can't give you any information about me."

It seems the world will never know what happened to Jody Roberts back in 1985. We don't know how or why she ended up in Colorado. We don't know what made her forget—or want to forget—her old life. We only know that the old Jody Roberts is gone. In her place is a woman named Jane Dee.

If you have been timed while reading this article, enter your reading time below. Then turn to the Words-per-Minute Table on page 120 and look up your reading speed (words per minute). Enter your reading speed on the graph on page 121.

Reading Time: Selection 2

_____ : _____
MINUTES   SECONDS

UNDERSTANDING IDEAS Circle the letter of the best answer.

1. **How did Jody Roberts' mystery begin?**
   A An injury wiped out her memory.
   B She did not show up for work one day.
   C Her parents didn't know where she was.
   D She turned up in a Colorado shopping mall.

2. **According to doctors, what might have caused Jody's amnesia?**
   F No one recognized her.
   G She carried no identification.
   H She drank a lot and was unhappy.
   J She may have suffered a terrible shock.

3. **Because Jody had closed her bank account before vanishing, some people believe that she was**
   A writing a story
   B faking amnesia
   C planning a trip
   D telling the truth

4. **Which of the following would Jody most likely remember?**

F the U. S. president
G the name of her mother
H her first birthday party
J her high school graduation

SUMMARIZE For each blank, choose the word that best completes the meaning of the paragraph.

mystery	disappeared	
		amnesia
information	doctors	

One day an unhappy reporter named Jody Roberts

_____. Five days later,

a woman who had _____

was found in Colorado. Named Jane Dee by

_____, she later moved to

Alaska, married a fisherman, and had children. She could

not recall any _____ about her

old life. What made Jody forget her previous life is still

a _____.

IF YOU WERE THERE Write a brief paragraph explaining what you would you do if you were Jody's best friend. Be sure to include examples from the story to support your response.

_____

_____

_____

_____

_____

_____

_____

USE CONTEXT CLUES When you read, you may find a word whose meaning is unfamiliar to you. When that happens, you can look up the word's meaning in the dictionary. You can also find out what the word means by looking for context clues. These are words or sentences that come before or after the word. Context clues can be words with the same or opposite meanings as the unfamiliar word. They may also be an example or definition of the unfamiliar word.

Read each excerpt from the stories you just read. Circle the letter with the best meaning of the underlined word.

1. **Suddenly, Krickitt swerved to avoid a slow-moving truck. She didn't turn fast enough and hit the back of the truck.**

   A went without warning

   B stopped moving

   C moved fast in a straight line

   D turned aside from a straight course

2. **Krickitt had amnesia. The blow to her brain had wiped out all her recent memories. She couldn't remember anything about the last 18 months.**

   F brain repairs

   G bad accident

   H shocking pain

   J loss of memory

3. **The head injuries left her more outgoing but also more temperamental. She often got angry.**

   A crazy

   B funny

   C lively

   D moody

4. **Her parents didn't know where she was. Neither did her sisters, brothers, or friends. It was as though the 26-year-old reporter had vanished into thin air.**

   F disappeared

   G enlightened

   H forgotten

   J reported

5. **She had no idea who she was. She couldn't remember how she got to the mall. Her pockets contained no identification.**

   A money to pay bills

   B things to write about

   C means of finding out who she was

   D ways of remembering where she was

PUT WORDS INTO CONTEXT Complete the paragraph using the underlined words from the exercise on this page.

When you lose the ability to remember, you may be

suffering from _____.

This condition can cause you to be emotional or

_____. Imagine finding yourself

lost with no _____. You would

feel as if your past had _____.

MAKE ROOT CONNECTIONS One way of finding out the meaning of a word is by looking for its root. An unfamiliar word may share a common root with a word that you know. A root is a part of many different words and may not be a word by itself. The root *mem*, for example, comes from a Latin word that means "keep in mind." You will find it in the words *memory* and *remember*.

Underline the root that connects each group of words. Then choose the best meaning of the root.

1. **reporter, support, portable**
   A to carry
   B to put
   C a gate
   D left side

2. **television, visualize, revisit**
   F to tell
   G to see
   H eyes
   J calls

3. **pressure, oppression, depress**
   A rest
   B sure
   C to force
   D to iron

4. **apartment, partition, department**
   F a way of gathering socially
   G to use skill and imagination
   H a score equal to the standard
   J to become separated into parts

5. **minimum, miniature, diminish**
   A second
   B hour
   C small
   D tight

ROOT ANALOGIES Analogies show similar patterns and relationships between words. Root analogies show relationships between words that have the same root word. For example, *use* is to *useable* as *move* is to *moveable*. Both root words, when combined with *able*, make a new word. For each blank, choose one of the boldfaced words from the exercise on this page to correctly complete the analogy.

1. *Mem* is to *memorize* as *vis* is to

   _____ .

2. *Part* is to *depart* as *press* is to

   _____ .

3. *Form* is to *reformer* as *port* is to

   _____ .

4. *Sign* is to *signature* as *mini* is to

   _____ .

5. *Ami* is to *amiable* as *port* is to

   _____ .

ORGANIZE THE FACTS The two stories you read in this unit are alike in some ways and different in other ways. A Venn diagram can show how they are alike and different. Look at the Venn diagram below. Then choose the best answer to each question.

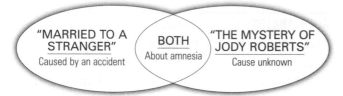

"MARRIED TO A STRANGER"
Caused by an accident

BOTH
About amnesia

"THE MYSTERY OF JODY ROBERTS"
Cause unknown

1. **Which detail about the main character does NOT belong in the oval marked "BOTH"?**

   A adjusts to life with amnesia

   B remembers part of her past

   C turned up in Colorado

   D memories never came back

2. **Which detail does NOT belong in the oval marked "Married to a Stranger"?**

   F Everyone believed that the main character had amnesia.

   G The main character and her husband fell in love again.

   H The main character was very happy before having amnesia.

   J Friends were surprised when the main character vanished.

3. **Which detail does NOT belong in the oval marked "The Mystery of Jody Roberts"?**

   A The main character did not recognize her husband.

   B The main character was unhappy before having amnesia.

   C The police thought that the main character had been murdered.

   D Some people believed that the main character was faking amnesia.

4. **Which detail belongs in the oval marked "BOTH"?**

   F The main character gets professional help.

   G The main character gets married a second time.

   H Doctors think the memory loss is temporary.

   J Friends help the main character remember her past.

PROVE THE COMPARISON AND CONTRAST Compare and contrast the two stories by writing sentences that support the topic sentence below.

The two stories are alike in some ways, but different in other ways.

_____

_____

_____

_____

_____

_____

_____

FACT AND OPINION

FACT AND OPINION A statement of fact is one that you can prove to be true. An opinion is a belief or conclusion that is still open to debate.

Read this passage about amnesia. Then choose the best answer to each question.

[1] One common cause of amnesia is aging. [2] As people grow older, the delivery of blood and nutrients to brain cells may diminish. [3] Why, for example, can many older people recall their high school days but can't remember what they ate for breakfast? [4] Perhaps the small portions of their brains that keep recent memories have died.

1. **Which sentence from the passage states a fact about the cause of amnesia?**
   A Sentence 1
   B Sentence 2
   C Sentence 3
   D Sentence 4

2. **Which sentence from the passage states an opinion about loss of recent memory?**
   F Sentence 1
   G Sentence 2
   H Sentence 3
   J Sentence 4

3. **Which sentence from the passage asks for a factual reason for memory loss in older people?**
   A Sentence 1
   B Sentence 2
   C Sentence 3
   D Sentence 4

JUDGE THE EVIDENCE

JUDGE THE EVIDENCE To convince a reader to agree to an opinion, the writer often provides evidence. The reader has to judge if the evidence is adequate to support the opinion. Choose the best answer.

1. **Which statement best supports the opinion that drinking alcohol can cause amnesia?**
   A Injuries to the head are often caused by drinking alcohol.
   B People who drink too much want to forget an unhappy event.
   C Heavy drinkers can't recall what they did while they were drunk.
   D Older people who drink can remember events that took place years before.

2. **Which statement best supports the opinion that amnesia caused by head injury can be treated?**
   F As the injury to the brain heals, memory returns.
   G Injuries to the brain sometimes cause partial amnesia.
   H Drugs can cause a person to talk freely about his or her past.
   J Clues to a person's past may appear when a person is injured.

YOUR OPINION

YOUR OPINION Write a brief paragraph expressing your opinion about the causes of amnesia. Support your opinion with evidence from the stories you have read.

_____

_____

_____

_____

_____

Sleeping Their Lives Away

Anne Brown thought her daughter Kristie was getting the flu. That would explain why 16-year-old Kristie suddenly felt so tired. On September 18, 1993, Kristie came home from a friend's house. She was so exhausted she went straight to bed. She slept all that day and right through the night. It turned out that Kristie didn't have the flu. She just couldn't seem to stay awake. She slept just as much the next day . . . and the next . . . and the next . . . and the next. In fact, Kristie didn't really wake up until five months later.

Kristie Brown has a very rare sleeping disorder. It is called Kleine Levin Syndrome, or KLS for short. There are only about a hundred known cases of it in the world. Nobody knows what causes it and nobody knows how to cure it. All you can do is hope it doesn't strike you.

People with KLS typically get their first attack as teenagers. They may feel run-down for a day or two before it hits, or they may have no warning at all. In any case, they suddenly feel an overwhelming need to sleep. They just want to sleep every hour of the day. There is no way to predict how long an episode will last. It may be days, weeks, or months. During an episode, KLS patients sleep up to 23 hours a day. Even when they are not sleeping, they aren't really awake. They are drowsy and disoriented, as though in some sort of trance. They may appear scared or irritable, and their sense of taste and smell seems altered. When the attack ends, they don't have much memory of it. They feel as though they are coming out of a fog.

Taryn Sardis had her first episode when she was in high school. She fell asleep in class. "It was almost impossible to wake her up," her mother said. Taryn's father brought her home and put her to bed. That's where she stayed for the next week and a half. During that time, Taryn slept about 20 hours a day. "She wouldn't want to wash or brush her teeth, go to the bathroom, shower, or anything during this period," said her father. Sometimes she would talk, but her voice had an odd, sing-song quality.

Jeff Sagel had a similar experience. Jeff was 14 years old when he had his first attack in 1994. It lasted over a week. During much of that time Jeff didn't speak. When he did talk, he didn't make sense. He sang the same two songs over and over again. After he snapped out of it, he wasn't sure what had happened to him. He felt like he had been in some weird dream state.

Because KLS is so rare, most people have never heard of it. So parents rarely suspect the true cause of their child's sleepiness. Anne Brown thought her daughter had the flu. Taryn Sardis' parents wondered if their daughter had taken some sort of drug. And when Nicole Santi had her first attack, her parents thought she was just worn down. Nicole's attack came right after the Christmas holidays, when the 17-year-old high school senior had been busier than ever. Her parents knew it was strange for Nicole to sleep so many days in a row, but they hoped it was just a one-time case of exhaustion.

Doctors, too, have limited experience with KLS. They often fail to recognize the symptoms. At first Jeff Sagel's doctors thought he had a sinus infection. Then they thought he had swelling in his brain. One of Kristie Brown's doctors thought migraine headaches were to blame. Others suggested everything from depression to drug addiction.

When a KLS attack ends, patients return to normal. They sometimes have difficulty making up the schoolwork they have missed. And if the attack is a long one—like Kristie Brown's five-month episode—it may take a while for them to get their muscle strength back. Still, they feel like their old selves again.

Unfortunately, there's no way of knowing when the next attack will begin. Some patients seem to fall into patterns. For Nicole Santi, attacks tend to come every six months and usually last about a week and a half. For Spencer Spearin, the attacks are much more frequent. In the first 22 months, Spencer had twenty attacks, each about ten days long. Kristie Brown's attacks haven't followed a pattern. But in the first eight years with the disorder, she spent about half of her time sleeping. Essentially, she lost years of her life.

Doctors say that KLS sometimes goes away on its own as patients get older. But it takes ten or twenty years for that to happen—if it happens at all. Some people live with the disorder well into their 50s or beyond. All KLS patients hope that someday a cure can be found. But in the meantime, they do the best they can. As Taryn Sardis says, "I just have to deal with it one day at a time."

If you have been timed while reading this article, enter your reading time below. Then turn to the Words-per-Minute Table on page 120 and look up your reading speed (words per minute). Enter your reading speed on the graph on page 121.

Reading Time: Selection 1

_____ : _____
MINUTES   SECONDS

UNDERSTANDING IDEAS Circle the letter of the best answer.

1. **Why is Kleine-Levin Syndrome, or KLS, considered a rare sleeping disorder?**

   A There are only a hundred known cases of it in the world.

   B It makes people feel an overwhelming need to sleep.

   C Parents rarely suspect the true cause of their child's sleepiness.

   D Nobody knows what causes it, and nobody knows how to cure it.

2. **Most people with KLS have their first attack in their**

   F teens

   G twenties

   H forties

   J old age

3. **What happens after a KLS attack ends?**

   A Patients must stay under a doctor's care.

   B Patients start medication to prevent future attacks.

   C Patients return to normal.

   D Patients must go to physical therapy.

4. **Which of the following statements is FALSE?**

   F Doctors are often unfamiliar with KLS.

   G Most people have never heard of KLS.

   H Parents sometimes think their children are taking drugs.

   J KLS attacks don't usually last long.

5. **Based on the examples of KLS in the story, the reader can conclude that**

   A attacks fall in a very definite pattern

   B the disorder is simply a form of laziness

   C warnings can help a person deal with it

   D there is nothing a person can do to prevent it

SUMMARIZE For each blank, choose the word that best completes the meaning of the paragraph.

attack	trouble	
older	cure	disorder

KLS stands for Kleine-Levin Syndrome and is a rare sleeping _____. There is no _____ for it at this time. During a KLS _____, patients may sleep up to 23 hours a day. When patients come out of an attack, they may have _____ making up the work they missed. Doctors say that sometimes KLS goes away as patients get _____.

IF YOU WERE THERE Imagine that you have a friend with KLS. Write a brief paragraph explaining what you might do to help. Be sure to include examples from the story to support your response.

_____
_____
_____
_____
_____
_____

Sleep Eating

"I started doing it when I was 17," says 36-year-old Susan Scott. "Half asleep, I got out of bed one night, walked down the stairs to the refrigerator, and ate some leftover fried chicken."

Susan woke up while she was still in the kitchen. Puzzled, she just stumbled back to bed. The next morning, she didn't think too much about what had happened. She figured she'd just been hungry. Everyone likes a midnight snack once in a while.

But Susan's nighttime snacking was not a one-time occurrence. As time passed, she began doing it more often. Again and again she climbed out of bed in the middle of the night and headed for the kitchen. She ate large amounts of food and then returned to her room. In the morning, Susan would be surprised to see bread crumbs on the floor or an empty peanut butter jar on the counter. She had no idea she had been eating during the night. She'd been sound asleep the whole time.

Susan Scott suffers from a rare sleep disorder called "sleep eating." No one knows what causes it. Some doctors think it is like other eating disorders. They believe it comes from unhealthy attitudes toward food. "If you have a huge desire to eat, you could be compelled to sleep eat," says Professor Janet Treasure.

Others disagree. They believe the problem is more like sleepwalking. They think it may be triggered by stress. "This is a sleep disorder, not an eating disorder," declares Dr. Mark Mahowald.

Whatever the cause, sleep eating is extremely rare. Only about a hundred cases have been diagnosed. There may be more sufferers out there. They're just afraid to admit it.

Sleep eaters fall asleep like any normal person. But at some point in the night, they begin to stir. Their bodies wake up, but their minds stay asleep. In this state, they are able to perform all sorts of actions. Some make sandwiches or even cook meals. Yet they have no memory of any of this because their conscious minds are sleeping.

Sleep eaters consume large amounts of food during these times. Marilyn Faber, a Minnesota woman, describes waking up after a night of eating. "I would maybe find a pork chop bone in the bed, tubs of sour cream in my bed . . ."

Angie Robinson from North Carolina knows what that is like. "I've woken up choking on food, with pork chops in my bed, and Snickers melted in my hair," she says.

Sleep eaters seem to prefer foods that contain a lot of sugar or fat. They love brownies, potato chips, or greasy donuts. Says Ryan Pruitt of Raleigh,

North Carolina, "If we've got cereal, I eat cereal. If it's cookies, I'll eat cookies. Anything chocolatey or sweet; anything with lots of sugar." But if sweets are not available, sleep eaters will eat whatever they can find. They'll eat prunes, onions, mayonnaise, or raw potatoes. They've been known to eat sticks of butter, raw bacon, even cat food.

Needless to say, sleep eaters have trouble staying thin. They may watch what they eat during the day, but when they are sleep eating, they show no self-control. Ryan Pruitt says he has gained 35 to 40 pounds. And Susan Scott has gone up two dress sizes. Sleep eaters also worry about swallowing something dangerous. "I worry one day I'll eat something really harmful," says Angie Robinson.

Sleep eaters don't enjoy their nighttime habit. Most of them try all sorts of ways to stop. Some hide food or have their spouses hide it. Some try not to keep any goodies in the house. Marilyn Faber has tried taping her refrigerator shut. Susan Scott has put a lock on her refrigerator. Ryan Pruitt even tried tying himself to his bed before going to sleep.

None of these plans work. Sleep eaters will break locks. They will pry open sealed containers. They will search room after room, looking for food. And if they can't find food, they will eat whatever they do find. Susan Scott once ate a bottle of Tums pills because they were fruit flavored. Says Angie Robinson, "I think I once drank a bit of liquid detergent as I could smell it on me the next morning and I was sick for three days."

Doctors don't know how to cure sleep eaters. Some doctors prescribe sleeping pills. Some offer counseling. Some suggest support groups. Marilyn Faber got her sleep eating under control through medication. But medicines don't work for everyone. Until more is learned about this disorder, many sleep eaters will keep making their nightly raids on everything from chocolate bars to soap.

If you have been timed while reading this article, enter your reading time below. Then turn to the Words-per-Minute Table on page 120 and look up your reading speed (words per minute). Enter your reading speed on the graph on page 121.

Reading Time: Selection 2

_____ : _____
MINUTES   SECONDS

UNDERSTANDING IDEAS Circle the letter of the best answer.

1. **Which of the following statements is TRUE about Susan Scott?**

   A Sleep eating was a one-time occurrence for her.

   B She has been sleep eating since she was ten years old.

   C Susan has gone up two dress sizes because of sleep eating.

   D Susan always remembers if she got up to eat during the night.

2. **According to the story, Professor Janet Treasure believes that people who sleep eat**

   F are simply not eating enough during the day

   G have a huge desire to eat

   H suffer from a sleep disorder

   J are simply walking in their sleep

3. **During a sleep eating episode a sleep eater would**

   A often wake up while eating

   B not fall asleep like a normal person

   C always choke on large pieces of food

   D usually eat a large quantity of food

4. **Based on the type of food that most sleep eaters prefer, which conclusion can you make?**

   F Sleep eaters prefer food that makes them fat.

   G The food they eat causes sleep eaters to choke.

   H The causes of sleep eating are in the refrigerator.

   J Sleep eaters consume the same food they eat all day.

5. **Which evidence proves that sleep eaters do not enjoy their habit?**

   A Some pry open sealed containers.

   B Doctors don't know how to cure them.

   C Most of them try all sorts of ways to stop.

   D They search room after room, looking for food.

SUMMARIZE For each blank, choose the word that best completes the meaning of the paragraph.

control	discouraged	
eating	sleepwalking	rare

Sleep eating is a _____

disorder. Some doctors think that it is an

_____ disorder, not a sleep

disorder. Other doctors think that it is more closely

related to _____. Sleep eaters

are unable to _____

themselves during an episode. They are often

_____ to wake up and find out

how much they have eaten.

IF YOU WERE THERE Write a brief paragraph explaining what you would do if you had this problem or one like it. Be sure to include examples from the story to support your response.

_____

_____

_____

_____

_____

_____

_____

MULTIPLE MEANINGS Often, words have more than one meaning. When you read a word with multiple meanings, you must look at the context of the sentence to determine the correct meaning. What that means is you must look for clues from the words surrounding the multiple-meaning word so you can determine what the correct definition is.

attack:	**1.** a fit of sickness; **2.** a hostile action; **3.** the act of attacking with physical force; **4.** a scoring action
case:	**1.** a box for holding something; **2.** a suit or action in law; **3.** an instance of disease or injury; **4.** what actually exists or happens: fact
jar:	**1.** to make a harsh sound; **2.** to make unstable: shake; **3.** a wide mouthed container made typically of earthenware or glass; **4.** a state of conflict
sound:	**1.** free from error; **2.** deep and undisturbed; **3.** showing good judgment; **4.** solid, firm
strike:	**1.** to take a course (as in a path); **2.** to deliver a blow (as with the hand); **3.** to engage in battle; **4.** to hit (to come into contact forcefully)

Read each excerpt from the stories you just read. Then choose the correct meaning of the underlined word, based on its use in the sentence. Use the dictionary entries above.

1. **There are only about a hundred known cases of it [KLS] in the world.**
   A Meaning 1
   B Meaning 2
   C Meaning 3
   D Meaning 4

2. **All you can do is hope it [KLS] doesn't strike you.**
   F Meaning 1
   G Meaning 2
   H Meaning 3
   J Meaning 4

3. **Jeff was 14 years old when he had his first attack in 1994.**
   A Meaning 1
   B Meaning 2
   C Meaning 3
   D Meaning 4

4. **Susan would be surprised to see bread crumbs on the floor or an empty peanut butter jar on the counter.**
   F Meaning 1
   G Meaning 2
   H Meaning 3
   J Meaning 4

5. **She'd been sound asleep the whole time.**
   A Meaning 1
   B Meaning 2
   C Meaning 3
   D Meaning 4

PUT WORDS INTO CONTEXT Complete the paragraph using the underlined words from the exercise on this page.

During one sleep eating _____,

a sleep eater had a choice between a bowl of carrots

and a _____ of marmalade.

Guess which food would be chosen in such

_____? The person may be

_____ asleep, but he or she

would choose anything high in fat or sugar when the

urge _____.

PREFIXES A prefix is one or more letters added to the beginning of a word to change its meaning. For example, the prefix *non-* means "not." The word *toxic* means "poisonous." So when you add the prefix *non-* to the beginning of the word *toxic*, you get *nontoxic*, which means "not poisonous."

Use a dictionary to find the meaning of each prefix below. Match the prefix with its meaning on the right. Write the letter of the correct definition on the line. **One of the letters will be used twice.**

_____ **1.** mis-   **A** do the opposite of

_____ **2.** un-   **B** the part in the middle

_____ **3.** re-   **C** badly, wrongly

_____ **4.** dis-   **D** again

_____ **5.** mid-   **E** against

_____ **6.** in-   **F** not

_____ **7.** pre-   **G** before

_____ **8.** anti-

WRITE DEFINITIONS For the below exercise, underline the prefix and write the meaning of the word on the line provided.

1. in + experience = inexperience

definition: _____

2. un + fortunately = unfortunately

definition: _____

3. dis + order = disorder

definition: _____

4. mid + night = midnight

definition: _____

5. un + healthy = unhealthy

definition: _____

6. mis + diagnosed = misdiagnosed

definition: _____

7. un + conscious = unconscious

definition: _____

8. dis + agree = disagree

definition: _____

<u>ORGANIZE THE FACTS</u> The two stories you read in this unit are alike in some ways and different in other ways. A Venn diagram can show how they are alike and different. Look at the Venn diagram below. Then choose the best answer to each question.

"SLEEPING THEIR LIVES AWAY"
Overwhelming need to sleep

BOTH
Very rare disorder

"SLEEP EATING"
Uncontrollable eating while asleep

1. **Which of the following details belongs in the oval marked "BOTH"?**

   A   may have trouble staying thin

   B   may appear at first to be drug addiction

   C   can sleep up to 23 hours a day during an attack

   D   about a hundred known cases of the disorder in the world

2. **Which detail does NOT belong in the oval marked "Sleeping Their Lives Away"?**

   F   The disorder can affect muscle strength.

   G   Kristie's mother thought she was getting the flu.

   H   This disorder may be an eating disorder, not a sleeping disorder.

   J   Patients may have terrible difficulty catching up with missed work.

3. **Which detail does NOT belong in the oval marked "Sleep Eating"?**

   A   Patients may even cook meals during an episode.

   B   Taryn Sardis had her first attack in high school.

   C   Susan's nighttime snacking happened often.

   D   Patients worry about swallowing something dangerous.

4. **Which detail belongs in the oval marked "BOTH"?**

   F   starts with tiredness

   G   nobody knows the cause

   H   goes away when one gets older

   J   patients feel like they have the flu

<u>CONTINUE THE COMPARISON</u> Fill in the chart with four additional details about how the stories are alike.

More ways the stories are alike:

FACT AND OPINION Facts and opinions can sometimes be hard to tell apart. People often represent opinion as if it were fact. To tell if something is a fact or opinion, determine whether what is being said is something that can be proven to be true. If it can, it's a fact. If not, it's someone's opinion.

Read this passage about another sleep disorder called narcolepsy. Then choose the best answer to each question.

[1] Another sleep disorder with no known cause or cure is narcolepsy. [2] People with narcolepsy fall asleep during the day, even when they want to stay awake. [3] It doesn't even matter if they had a full night's sleep the night before. [4] Can you imagine how dangerous this sleep disorder is if it strikes while you are driving? [5] People with narcolepsy are probably frustrated a lot of the time. [6] While KLS and sleep eating are extremely rare, narcolepsy affects about 50,000 people in the United States alone.

1. **Which sentence from the paragraph states a FACT about <u>when</u> people are affected by narcolepsy?**

   A Sentence 1

   B Sentence 2

   C Sentence 3

   D Sentence 4

2. **Which sentence from the paragraph states an OPINION about people with narcolepsy?**

   F Sentence 3

   G Sentence 4

   H Sentence 5

   J Sentence 6

JUDGE THE EVIDENCE Think back to what you have read. Review the paragraph about narcolepsy on this page. Then choose the best answer.

1. **Which of the following statements is TRUE?**

   A All three sleep disorders affect roughly the same number of people.

   B No one knows the causes of the three sleep disorders.

   C Most people who have sleep disorders are men.

   D Patients who have narcolepsy likely have another sleeping disorder, too.

2. **Which of the following statements is FALSE?**

   F Of the three sleep disorders you've just read about, narcolepsy affects the largest number of people.

   G None of the sleep disorders in this unit have a cure.

   H Eventually, patients can outgrow all three sleep disorders.

   J Each of the sleep disorders makes it difficult to live a normal life.

JUST THE FACTS Fill in the chart below with FACTS about KLS and sleep eating. Make sure you do not include opinions.

KLS (Kleine-Levin Syndrome)

Sleep Eating

SELECTION 1
Evil Aliens

Kelly Cahill didn't believe in aliens. She didn't believe in UFOs or visitors from outer space. Kelly lived in Gippsland, Australia, with her husband Andrew and three young children.

On August 7, 1993, something happened that changed Kelly Cahill's life forever. She and Andrew were driving home from a friend's house when suddenly Kelly saw a lighted object in the sky ahead of them. Andrew saw it, too. Driving closer, they realized that it was some sort of spacecraft. Kelly saw creatures or "beings" standing in the windows.

As the Cahills watched in amazement, the object flew off to their left and disappeared. But half a mile down the road, a light appeared ahead of them. The light was so bright that Kelly had to shield her eyes with her hand. The light covered the entire road. There seemed to be no way around it. Kelly felt her pulse racing. She was starting to panic. "What are you going to do?" she cried out to Andrew.

"I will keep driving," he said. And so, moving at a speed of 60 miles per hour, the Cahills charged toward the light.

And then . . . nothing. The next thing Kelly knew, the light was gone. So was the sense of panic. The Cahills were moving along at 25 miles per hour.

"What happened?" Kelly asked Andrew. "I swear I had a blackout."

Andrew told her to forget about it. He said they had gone around a corner, that was all. He just wanted to forget the whole thing.

When they got home, Kelly looked at the clock. The one-and-a-half hour drive had taken them three hours. Kelly was alarmed by the "missing" time. She was also alarmed by the stomach pains that both she and Andrew experienced over the next several days.

Still, Kelly tried to follow Andrew's suggestion. She tried to forget the whole thing. And for a while she succeeded. But on October 1, as she and Andrew drove that same road again, the images and experiences of August 7th started to come back to her.

"As we passed the spot, my stomach [sank] with a sensation I can only describe as gut-wrenching dread," Kelly said. "The memories of that night came flooding back as clear as daylight. It was as if a secret door had been unlocked."

Kelly suddenly realized what had happened that night back in August. She had asked Andrew to stop the car. After he had pulled over, she'd noticed another car on the road behind them. It had also pulled to the side of the road and stopped.

Both Kelly and Andrew had stepped out of their car. "From nowhere appeared a tall dark figure," Kelly remembered. "I knew it was too tall to be human." The seven-foot creature was completely black except for its huge, fiery, red eyes. Soon it was joined by several other identical creatures. Kelly was terrified. She saw some of the creatures coming toward her and Andrew. Others headed toward the people in the car behind her.

Then Kelly had felt a blow to her stomach. She fell backwards, screaming out in fear and pain. "I was severely winded and nauseous and felt as if I was going to pass out," she recalled. She heard her husband shouting to the creatures to release him.

"How dare you do this to innocent people?" Kelly had screamed. "Get out of here and go back where you came from!"

That was all that Kelly remembered. Her next memory was of sitting in the car next to Andrew, moving along at 25 miles per hour.

Once these memories came back to Kelly, she didn't know what to do. When she tried to discuss them with Andrew, he became very upset. He didn't want to discuss anything about the night of August 7.

Finally, Kelly went to a UFO researcher named Bill Chalker. He put her in touch with a group called Phenomena Research Australia. Members of this group began investigating Kelly's story. The researchers went to the location where Kelly said her encounter with the creatures had taken place. They discovered an odd, crescent-shaped hollow in the earth. They noticed dead grass in the shape of a triangle. They also measured a high level of sulphur in the dirt.

That wasn't all. Kelly had said there was a second car on the road that night. The researchers put ads in the local papers to find the occupants of this car. After much effort, they succeeded. A bank manager, his wife, and their friend finally came forward. These people didn't know Kelly or Andrew. But their story supported Kelly's. They didn't remember the creatures' fiery red eyes, but the rest of her description matched what they had seen.

After recalling what had happened that August night, Kelly's life changed dramatically. Her religious beliefs were badly shaken. Her marriage crumbled. In 1996, Kelly wrote a book about what had happened to her. She titled it *Encounter*.

While some people brush off her story as fantasy, Kelly remains convinced that she was abducted by aliens that night. And she is certain that the creatures were up to no good. As she told one reporter, "I still say to this day that what I encountered out there had the essence of pure evil."

If you have been timed while reading this article, enter your reading time below. Then turn to the Words-per-Minute Table on page 120 and look up your reading speed (words per minute). Enter your reading speed on the graph on page 121.

Reading Time: Selection 1

_____ : _____
MINUTES   SECONDS

UNDERSTANDING IDEAS Circle the letter of the best answer.

1. **On August 7, when the Cahills first saw the blinding light, what did Andrew say he would do?**

   A call for help

   B keep driving

   C turn the car around

   D pull over to the side of the road

2. **Why was Kelly Cahill alarmed when she looked at the clock upon arriving home that night?**

   F She and Andrew had stomach pains.

   G The time on the clock had not changed.

   H The bright light was on the face of the clock.

   J The 1 1/2 hour trip had actually taken 3 hours.

3. **Which statement belongs in the empty box?**

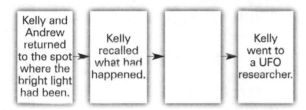

   A They were attacked by aliens.

   B Kelly wrote a book titled *Encounter*.

   C Researchers found the second car in the scene.

   D They had pulled to the side of the road and stopped.

4. **Which is the most convincing evidence that Kelly's story might be true?**

   F Kelly is the author of a book named *Encounter*.

   G The occupants of the second car supported her story.

   H The researchers noticed dead grass in the shape of a triangle.

   J Andrew remembered the events the same way Kelly did.

SUMMARIZE For each blank, choose the word that best completes the meaning of the paragraph.

abducted	remember	memories
driving	encountered	light

On August 7, 1993, Kelly and Andrew Cahill were

_____ home from a friend's

house when they _____

a blinding light on the road. The next thing they

_____ is driving along at

25 miles per hour. On October 1 that same year,

Kelly and Andrew drove by the same spot where the

_____ had been. All of Kelly's

_____ came back to her, and she

remembered being _____

by aliens.

IF YOU WERE THERE What would you have done if you were in the car with Andrew and Kelly the night they saw the bright light? Write a brief paragraph explaining your actions. Be sure to include examples from the story to support your response.

_____

_____

_____

_____

_____

Not Quite Human

Peter Khoury, 24 years old, was lying quietly on his bed in Sydney, Australia. His father and brother were dozing in the next room. Suddenly Peter felt someone—or something—grab him by the ankles. He tried to move but couldn't. He couldn't kick, couldn't twist, couldn't even cry out. His whole body was numb. The only thing he could move was his eyes.

Looking to his right, Peter saw several dark figures standing beside him. They were wearing dark robes and had hoods over their heads. "Their faces were very wrinkled and shiny dark black in color," Peter later said. "They were only about three to four feet in height."

Peter was terrified. As he lay there, the creatures began to talk to him—but without using voices. Somehow they were communicating telepathically. Their thoughts were going directly into his head. "I was told not to worry," Peter said. "I would not be harmed."

Peter rolled his eyes to the left. There he saw two more strange figures. These looked nothing like the little hooded creatures on his right. Instead, these beings were tall and thin and golden yellow, with big dark eyes and narrow chins. One of these creatures spoke to him. Again, the message passed telepathically. The creature told Peter not to worry—it would be "like the last time."

One of the yellow creatures put a long thin needle up against the left side of Peter's head. Peter was aware of the needle going in. Then he blacked out. When he woke up, he was alone in the room.

No longer numb, Peter jumped up off the bed and ran into the next room. He woke up his brother and father. They had not seen or heard anything. But although they believed they had only been dozing for ten minutes, they had really been asleep for two hours.

This event happened on July 12, 1988. The next day, Peter asked his future wife, Vivian, to look at his head. "I explained to her what had happened through the night," he said. "As I touched the spot where the needle was inserted, I discovered some dried blood under my fingernail."

Vivian took a look, and spotted a puncture mark on the left side of Peter's head. Alarmed, Peter went to see his family doctor. The doctor agreed that there was a puncture mark. But he said Peter must have hit his head on a nail. Peter tried to describe the creature with the needle, but the doctor just laughed.

For the next four years, Peter Khoury didn't talk much about his bizarre experience. It was just too weird for most people to accept.

Then, on July 23, 1993, Peter was visited by aliens for the second time. Once again he was in bed when it happened. This time there were just two creatures. Both were female. According to Peter, they looked a lot like humans but clearly weren't. For one thing, their faces were very long. Also, their eyes were two or three times as big as human eyes. "I have never seen a human looking like that," Peter later said. One of the visitors had straight black hair and dark skin. The other was light-skinned with blonde hair that went half-way down her back. This hair was curly, almost puffy. Peter described it as "exotic."

Again, Peter was frightened. But this time after the creatures left, he found something they had left behind: two strands of thin blonde hair. Realizing that the hairs were important evidence, he put them in a small plastic bag for safe-keeping.

For a long time, Peter kept the hairs sealed in the bag. He was reluctant to show them to anyone or to talk about his experience. At last, in 1996, he gave the hairs to the Anomaly Physical Evidence Group (APEG). This group investigates all sorts of claims about UFOs. The group is made up of scientists who want to remain anonymous. They are afraid their reputations would be hurt if people discovered they were doing UFO research.

APEG analyzed the two hairs. It ran DNA tests on them. Then it announced its conclusions. The hairs were very much like human hair—but not exactly. There were a few differences in the DNA. Only four people on Earth were known to have these differences. All four had a rare blend of Chinese and Mongolian ancestors. All four were Asian in appearance—meaning that their hair was black, not blonde. The hairs Peter supplied had not been dyed or colored in any way. As far as APEG knew, there was no one on Earth whose hair matched these samples.

The truth about the blonde hairs remains a mystery. Some people doubt the conclusions of APEG. Others think Peter Khoury made up his tales of alien visitors. They wonder where he really got the blonde hairs—or if the hairs even exist at all. But until more is discovered about this bizarre case, Peter Khoury's story fits squarely into the "unexplained" category.

If you have been timed while reading this article, enter your reading time below. Then turn to the Words-per-Minute Table on page 120 and look up your reading speed (words per minute). Enter your reading speed on the graph on page 121.

Reading Time: Selection 2

_____ : _____
MINUTES   SECONDS

UNDERSTANDING IDEAS Circle the letter of the best answer.

1. **Which picture best describes where Peter Khoury was the first time he says the alien creatures visited him?**

   A   bed

   B   car

   C   yard

   D   couch

2. **According to Peter, how did the aliens communicate with him?**

   F   They spoke to him.

   G   They used a mechanical translator.

   H   They did not communicate with him at all.

   J   They put their thoughts directly into Peter's head.

3. **What convinced Peter that the creatures really existed?**

   A   The aliens visited him a second time.

   B   They looked like humans but clearly weren't.

   C   There was a puncture on the side of his head where they had inserted a needle.

   D   His brother and father who were dozing in the next room heard him scream.

4. **Based on the DNA studies of the blonde hairs that Peter found, which inference can you make?**

   F   The hairs were exactly like human hair.

   G   Similar hairs on Earth have not been found.

   H   The hairs were once black and were dyed blonde.

   J   They can easily be recreated in a laboratory.

SUMMARIZE For each blank, choose the word that best completes the meaning of the paragraph.

female	aliens	hairs	two
worry	telepathically	inserted	

Peter Khoury says he was visited by

_____ who communicated with

him _____. They told him that he

should not _____. But then,

the aliens _____ a long needle

into Peter's head, and he blacked out. The second time

he was visited by aliens, there were only

_____ of them, and they were

both _____. Peter saved two

blonde _____ that one of the

aliens left behind.

IF YOU WERE THERE Imagine that you are Peter Khoury. How would you describe the event to your fiancée Vivian? Write a brief paragraph explaining what you would tell her after the first visit by the aliens. Be sure to include examples from the story to support your response.

_____

_____

_____

_____

_____

_____

USE CONTEXT CLUES When you read, you may find a word whose meaning is unfamiliar to you. When that happens, you can look up the word's meaning in the dictionary. You can also find out what the word means by looking for context clues. These are words or sentences that come before or after the word. Context clues can be words with the same or opposite meanings as the unfamiliar word. They may also be an example or definition of the unfamiliar word.

Read each excerpt from the stories you just read. Circle the letter with the best meaning of the underlined word.

1. "As we passed the spot, my stomach [sank] with a <u>sensation</u> I can only describe as gut-wrenching dread."

   A sickness

   B pain

   C thought

   D feeling

2. The seven-foot creature was completely black except for its huge, fiery, red eyes. Soon it was joined by several other <u>identical</u> creatures.

   F tall

   G exactly alike

   H evil-looking

   J hairy

3. "I was severely winded and <u>nauseous</u> and felt as if I was going to pass out."

   A sick

   B tired

   C hurt

   D afraid

4. Peter kept the hairs sealed in a bag. He was <u>reluctant</u> to show them to anyone or to talk about his experience.

   F embarrassed

   G excited

   H unwilling

   J eager

5. The group is made up of scientists who want to remain <u>anonymous</u>. They are afraid their reputations would be hurt if people discovered they were doing UFO research.

   A famous

   B together

   C unknown

   D apart

6. But until more is discovered about this <u>bizarre</u> case, Peter Khoury's story fits squarely into the "unexplained" category.

   F awesome

   G exciting

   H scary

   J weird

PUT WORDS INTO CONTEXT Complete the paragraph using the underlined words from the exercise on this page.

If you think you have had an alien experience, you may be _____ to talk about it because someone might laugh at you. If you do talk about it, you may want to remain _____ and not use your real name. Many people who say they have been visited by aliens describe nearly _____ beings. So, you might be surprised at what you find if you talk to other people. Your story might not be as _____ as you think.

SUFFIXES A suffix is one or more letters added to the end of a word to change its meaning. For example, the suffix *–dom* means "a state of being." So, when you add the suffix *–dom* to the end of the word *free*, you get *freedom*, which means "the state of being free."

Use a dictionary to find the meaning of each suffix below. Match the suffix with its meaning on the right. Write the letter of the correct definition on the line. **One of the letters will be used twice.**

_____ **1.** -ly

_____ **2.** -ful

_____ **3.** -or

_____ **4.** -en

_____ **5.** -ant

_____ **6.** -er

_____ **7.** -less

_____ **8.** -ment

A one that performs (a specified action)

B a person who

C made of, consisting of

D in the manner of

E condition resulting from a (specified action)

F without

G characterized by

WRITE DEFINITIONS In the exercise below, underline the suffix and write the new meaning of the word on the line provided.

1. visit + or = visitor

definition: _____

2. account + ant = accountant

definition: _____

3. amaze + ment = amazement

definition: _____

4. complete + ly = completely

definition: _____

5. peace + ful = peaceful

definition: _____

6. friend + ly = friendly

definition: _____

7. research + er = researcher

definition: _____

8. gold + en = golden

definition: _____

FIND THE PURPOSE Authors write to inform or teach, to persuade or convince, or to entertain. Sometimes there may be more than one purpose for writing. One example of multipurpose writing is the movie review. The review informs the reader about the movie, but it often persuades the reader to see or not see the film. Reviewers may also entertain the reader by making the review funny if the movie lends itself to humor.

Look at the chart below. Then choose the best answer to each question.

AUTHOR'S PURPOSE		
to inform (teach)	to persuade (convince)	to entertain (amuse)
• textbook	• editorials	• fictional stories
• newspaper and magazine articles	• advertisements	• poems
• nonfiction stories/books	• position papers (for or against an issue)	• humorous essays, books, or cartoons
• reviews (movies, books, music, and so on)	• lawyer's briefs (arguments)	• anecdotes (personal stories)

1. **"Evil Aliens" is an example of a story that should appear under which heading?**
   A to inform
   B to persuade
   C to entertain
   D all of the above

2. **If "Not Quite Human" were an imaginary story, under which heading would it appear on the chart?**
   F to inform
   G to persuade
   H to entertain
   J all of the above

3. **A reviewer's recommendation of *Encounter* by Kelly Cahill should appear under which heading?**
   A to inform
   B to persuade
   C to entertain
   D all of the above

4. **An author writes a humorous essay stating the opinion that alien encounters are unbelievable. What two purposes does the author have?**
   F to entertain and to persuade
   G to inform and to entertain
   H to inform and to persuade
   J all of the above

WRITE WITH A PURPOSE Write a topic sentence for each of the purposes you have learned.

to inform: _____

_____

to persuade: _____

_____

to entertain: _____

_____

VERIFYING EVIDENCE As a reader, it's up to you to weigh the evidence being offered in any piece of writing. When the author has written to inform or persuade, you must verify or confirm the evidence being offered and judge just how believable that evidence is. Pretend you came across the following item in your daily newspaper. Read the article and then choose the best answer for each question.

[1] Martina Rassla reported today that four seven-foot-tall aliens visited last night in her home. [2] Rassla reported that the aliens asked for all the silver and gold in the house to use as fuel for their spaceship. [3] She said the aliens were not aggressive. [4] Rassla's husband, Anthony was home at the time of the incident. [5] "I saw four tall scary-lookin' dudes. [6] They scared me and Martina to death."

[7] Experts say that each year thousands of Americans report being visited by an alien being. [8] Some people have even tried taking pictures of the aliens. [9] Dr. Jack Taylor at the Alien Abduction Research Center said that "people are visited by aliens and often aren't aware of it. [10] They attribute the strange noises to the wind or a passing car, rather than the true source."

1. Which is the best source for verifying what experts have said?

A a supermarket tabloid

B the encyclopedia

C your community newsletter

D the monthly magazine *Aliens Are Here*

2. Which of the following sentences offers the most convincing evidence that Martina Rassla might be telling the truth?

F Sentences 1 and 2

G Sentences 3 and 4

H Sentences 5–7

J Sentences 8–10

JUDGE THE EVIDENCE To persuade the reader of an opinion or story, the author often provides evidence. It is up to the reader to judge if the evidence presented is believable or not.

1. Which statement best supports the opinion that aliens have had contact with humans?

A Crop circles are common in the Midwest.

B Each year, thousands of people say they've had alien encounters.

C Some people appear to have alien implants on their foreheads.

D People have seen pictures in magazines of alien spaceships.

2. Which statement best supports Peter Khoury's story from "Not Quite Human"?

F Peter felt a presence in the room that paralyzed him.

G The Anomaly Physical Evidence Group concluded that the hairs Peter gave them to study did not match any human hair on Earth.

H Peter's fiancée Vivian saw that Peter had a puncture wound on his head.

J Peter says he was visited twice by aliens, once in 1988 and once in 1993.

PERSUADE WITH EVIDENCE Write two sentences persuading your reader about a strange thing that has happened to you. The first sentence should summarize your story. The second sentence should try to prove that your story is true.

_____

_____

_____

_____

SELECTION 1

They Saw It Coming

Mrs. Philip Straub was going on a picnic. On June 15, 1904, she boarded a ship called the *General Slocum*. More than 1,300 people joined her. They planned to leave New York City around 9 A.M. They were going to sail up the East River to the Locust Grove Picnic Grounds. Everyone was looking forward to a wonderful outing. But just before the ship sailed, Mrs. Straub felt a sudden stab of fear. She became convinced that the *General Slocum* was headed for disaster. Pushing through the crowd, she hurried down the gangplank. Just a few minutes later, the ship sailed without her.

Mrs. Straub had experienced a premonition, or a feeling that something bad is about to happen. The feeling isn't based on facts. It's more like a hunch. Sometimes premonitions take the form of dreams. Others come while a person is wide awake.

No one knows for sure how or why premonitions occur. Some people think that time is being scrambled. They say premonitions offer real glimpses into the future. Other people think premonitions are just the result of ordinary fears and worries. In any case, those who ignore premonitions do so at their own peril.

Mrs. Straub acted on her premonition. And it was a good thing she did. Forty minutes after leaving shore, the *General Slocum* burst into flames. Over a thousand passengers died in the fire.

Years later, actress Lindsay Wagner had a similar experience. On May 25, 1979, Wagner and her mother were at the Chicago airport. They had tickets for an American Airlines flight. Ten minutes before takeoff, Wagner suddenly felt sick. She knew she had to get off that airplane. Both she and her mother rushed back into the airport. The plane took off without them. Just seconds after leaving the runway, it crashed. All 270 people on board were killed.

Sonya Baladi didn't have any bad feelings about the flight she was going to take. But her mother did. Sonya had booked a seat on EgyptAir Flight 990. It was due to leave New York on October 31, 1999. But the day before the flight, Sonya's mother Laila had a premonition. She told Sonya it was not safe to get on the plane. Sonya listened to her mother. She canceled her plans. So she was on the ground when Flight 990 crashed in the Atlantic, killing everyone on board.

Roberto Clemente, Jr., wished that his father had listened to him. In December 1972, six-year-old Roberto begged his father not to fly. Roberto Clemente, Sr., was one of the greatest baseball players who ever lived. He was also a great human being. Clemente was headed to

Nicaragua to help earthquake victims there. Young Roberto didn't want him to go. "I had a feeling that the plane was going to crash," Roberto later said. "I asked him not to go. I went right between Mom and Dad and said, 'Don't get on that plane, it's going to crash.'" Sadly, Clemente didn't listen. The plane did crash, killing all five people on board.

Russian sailor Alexei Korkin is another person who might still be alive if he had heeded a premonition. In 2000, Alexei was 19 years old. He was stationed on the Russian submarine *Kursk*. One day he wrote a letter to a friend. He described a bad feeling he had. "I have all kinds of nightmares," he wrote. "It's good we're at our base, not at sea. We would sink, that's for sure." Alexei also wrote, "I have this premonition that the world is caving in, that everything is crumbling. . . . I have this feeling that something inevitable is going to happen."

On August 14, Alexei's premonition came true. The *Kursk* was in the Barents Sea with Alexei and 117 others on board. Suddenly, something went wrong. An explosion rocked the *Kursk*. The submarine sank to the ocean floor. Many crew members died right away. The rest were trapped without much oxygen. Rescuers did their best. But by the time they opened the *Kursk*, everyone inside was dead.

Johnny Horton's story is perhaps the saddest of all. Horton was a famous country singer. In the 1950s, he had one big hit after another. But in late 1960, Horton got a strong premonition. He felt he was in terrible danger. Horton told his band members about it. He said he thought a drunk was going to kill him.

Horton took this premonition seriously. He contacted his sister. He asked her to take care of his wife and two little daughters if he was killed. He also arranged to have his mother come for a visit. He wanted to see her one last time.

Horton then tried to cancel his next two appearances. He got out of one. But he couldn't cancel his show at the Skyline Club in Dallas, Texas. He had to sing there on November 4. Reluctantly, Horton went. He did his best to protect himself. When he wasn't on stage, he stayed in his dressing room. He refused to go anywhere near the bar. He figured that was where most of the drunks would be.

When it was time to go home, Horton was very relieved. It looked like his fears had been groundless. He got behind the wheel of his white Cadillac and began driving toward his home in Shreveport, Louisiana. By 2 A.M., he was near Milano, Texas. But as he drove across a bridge, an oncoming truck crossed the center line. It smashed right into him. Horton died on the way to the hospital. He had been killed by a drunk driver.

If you have been timed while reading this article, enter your reading time below. Then turn to the Words-per-Minute Table on page 120 and look up your reading speed (words per minute). Enter your reading speed on the graph on page 121.

Reading Time: Selection 1

_____ : _____
MINUTES   SECONDS

UNDERSTANDING IDEAS Circle the letter of the best answer.

1. **Why did Mrs. Straub leave just before the _General Slocum_ sailed?**

   A   She was going on a picnic.

   B   She hurried down the gangplank.

   C   She felt a sudden stab of fear.

   D   More than 1,300 people were onboard.

2. **In what way were the experiences of Sonya Baladi and Lindsay Wagner alike?**

   F   They both left the airplane just before it took off.

   G   They both had visions that they would be in a plane crash.

   H   They were both killed because they didn't listen to warnings.

   J   They both acted on premonitions and were saved from crashes.

3. **The episodes about Roberto Clemente, Sr., and Alexoi Korkin were both presented to prove which statement?**

   A   Those who ignore premonitions do so at their own peril.

   B   Premonitions are the result of ordinary fears and worries.

   C   When time is scrambled, people can see into the future.

   D   Sometimes premonitions take the form of dreams or feelings.

4. **What can you conclude from the Johnny Horton story?**

   F   He made sure his wife and two daughters were safe.

   G   He did not do enough to protect himself from a drunk killer.

   H   He performed at the Skyline Club often.

   J   His premonition was correct, but he didn't think that the killer would be a drunk driver.

SUMMARIZE For each blank, choose the word that best completes the meaning of the paragraph.

seconds	flight	rushed
fly	upcoming	premonition

A _____ is a feeling that

something bad is about to happen. Many people

believe they have had these warnings about

_____ disasters. For example,

Lindsay Wagner was on an American Airlines

_____ and got sick before takeoff.

She _____ off the plane, and

missed her flight. Just a few _____

after takeoff, the plane crashed. Roberto Clemente, Jr.,

asked his father not to _____ .

He flew anyway and the plane crashed.

IF YOU WERE THERE Have you ever had a premonition? If not, what would you do if you had one? Write a brief paragraph explaining what you might do. Be sure to include examples from the story to support your response.

_____

_____

_____

_____

A School Wiped Out

Alexander Venn had a feeling that trouble was coming. He didn't know exactly when or where. But he sensed that it would be a coal mining accident. And he sensed that it would occur near his home. "Something terrible is going to happen," he told his wife, "and it won't be far from here."

Venn wasn't the only one in Britain who had a premonition of disaster in October 1966. On October 20, Mrs. Sybil Brown had a disturbing dream. She saw children being swallowed up by a "black, billowing mass." She didn't know what it meant, but she couldn't shake the feeling that it was real.

That same day, Mary Hennessy also sensed impending doom. She dreamed of many schoolchildren gathered together in a big room. Something dreadful was happening to them. They were trying to get out of the room, but they were trapped. They began slipping out of sight. Hundreds of people came running to help. These rescuers looked horrified. "Some were crying and others holding handkerchiefs to their faces," said Mary. "It frightened me so much that it woke me up." Mary called her son and daughter-in-law and told them about her dream. She wanted to make sure her little granddaughters were okay.

Meanwhile, in Plymouth, England, Carolyn Miller was having a similar premonition. She was suddenly overcome by the image of an old schoolhouse. She saw an "avalanche of coal" flowing down a mountainside. A little boy stood at the bottom. He looked "absolutely terrified to death." Carolyn also saw rescue workers rushing about. She told her friends about the vision, but none of them knew quite what to make of it.

Miles away, in northwest England, a man dreamed of seven letters surrounded by bright lights. The letters spelled "A-B-E-R-F-A-N." The man had no idea what it meant. But he had the feeling his dream was trying to tell him something.

None of these people knew it, but their dreams and visions were all connected. The images were like pieces of a puzzle. Each one by itself made no sense. But taken together, they foretold the future. And they foretold it with frightening clarity.

Aberfan, it turned out, was the name of a small village in Wales. The village was not far from where Alexander Venn lived. In this village was a schoolhouse like the one Carolyn Miller saw in her vision. On October 21, a mountain of coal came crashing down upon this school, just as Carolyn had envisioned. As in Mary Hennessy's dream, the children inside had no chance to escape. They disappeared under what Sybil

Brown had called a "black, billowing mass" of coal.

It happened at 9:15 in the morning. A huge pile of coal collapsed on the mountainside above Aberfan. The pile was a "coal tip." It was made up of wet coal left over from local mining operations. When it collapsed, thousands of tons of coal came roaring down into the village. This river of coal was as wide as a three-lane highway. Moving at a speed of more than 20 miles an hour, it plowed directly into Pantglas Junior School.

Gaynor Madgwick was an eight-year-old student at the school. She had just gotten out of her seat when the wave of coal struck. She was swept away and ended up trapped under a radiator. "It was a horrible nightmare," she later said. "Bodies lay crushed and buried. I was too dazed to scream or do anything." Nine-year-old Gerald Kirwan was buried in coal up to his waist. "My best friend lay dead beside me," he remembered. Gerald and Gaynor survived until help arrived. But many of their classmates choked to death under the coal.

After the wave of coal hit, villagers rushed to the school. They began clawing away at the rubble. Most were digging with their bare hands. They managed to rescue ten children. But the other 116 students in the school died. So did 28 adults.

When people like Alexander Venn and Sybil Brown heard about the tragedy, they felt a shock of disbelief. Suddenly their dreams and visions made sense. Carolyn Miller turned on the TV to watch news reports from Aberfan. The camera showed the face of one boy rescued from the rubble. When Carolyn saw the boy, she gasped. She knew his face. It was the same little boy she had seen in her vision.

In London, a psychiatrist named John Barker heard about some of the Aberfan premonitions. Barker was intrigued. He decided to do a study. He only wanted to include genuine premonitions. So he looked for stories that could be verified. For instance, Carolyn Miller had told her friends about her vision the day before the tragedy. So it was clear that she was telling the truth.

In all, Dr. Barker found 24 cases he could verify. They came from all over Britain. One came from Aberfan itself. The day before the disaster, nine-year-old Eryl Mai Jones told her mother about a strange dream she'd had. She said, "I dreamed I went to school and there was no school there. Something black had come down all over it." Eryl Mai's mother didn't think much about it at the time. But the next day, when the disaster struck, Mrs. Jones realized what the dream meant. She hoped and prayed that her daughter would be found alive. But Eryl Mai, like so many others, died underneath the massive wave of coal.

If you have been timed while reading this article, enter your reading time below. Then turn to the Words-per-Minute Table on page 120 and look up your reading speed (words per minute). Enter your reading speed on the graph on page 121.

Reading Time: Selection 2

——————— : ———————
MINUTES   SECONDS

UNDERSTANDING IDEAS Circle the letter of the best answer.

1. In what way was Alexander Venn's premonition connected to the coal mining accident?

A He had seen frightened children in his dreams.

B As he had sensed, the accident happened near his home.

C He had told his wife about how the accident would occur.

D He was only one of several people who foresaw the accident.

2. When did the dreams and visions of the accident make sense to those who had them?

F as soon as they woke from the nightmares

G before they told anyone else about the dreams and visions

H after they heard about the tragedy at Pantglas Junior School

J when Dr. Barker asked them about their dreams and visions

3. How did Dr. John Barker verify Carolyn Miller's story?

A He knew that Carolyn always told the truth.

B He asked another doctor's opinion about her mind.

C He included her story in his study of the Aberfan premonitions.

D He asked her friends if she had talked about her vision before the tragedy.

4. Which statement would Dr. John Barker probably make after verifying 24 cases?

F In all 24 cases, a future disaster was foreseen.

G The tragedy could have been avoided if people listened.

H All 24 cases involved nightmares about school children.

J They all involved children who survived the accident.

SUMMARIZE For each blank, choose the word that best completes the meaning of the paragraph.

| village | escape | collapsed | school-children |
| disappear | correct | dreams | |

Several people had _____ and visions they didn't understand. One woman, Mary Hennessy, dreamed that _____ were trapped in a big room and couldn't _____. Then the children began to _____. Sadly, all of the premonitions were _____. On October 21, in a small _____ in Wales, a huge pile of coal _____ and slid down a mountain to the Pantglas Junior School, killing almost everyone inside.

IF YOU WERE THERE Imagine that you are one of the many people who had a premonition about the coal mining accident. Write a brief paragraph explaining how you would feel when you heard about the accident. Be sure to include examples from the story to support your response.

_____
_____
_____
_____
_____

USE CONTEXT CLUES When you read, you may find a word whose meaning is unfamiliar to you. When that happens, you can look up the word's meaning in the dictionary. You can also find out what the word means by looking for context clues. These are words or sentences that come before or after the word. Context clues can be words with the same or opposite meanings as the unfamiliar word. They may also be an example or definition of the unfamiliar word.

Read each excerpt from the stories you just read. Circle the letter of the best meaning of the underlined word.

1. The feeling isn't based on facts. It's more like a **hunch**.
   A something someone told you
   B made-up story
   C hint of a future event
   D wish for something

2. In any case, those who ignore premonitions do so at their own **peril**. Mrs. Straub acted on her premonition. And it was a good thing she did.
   F wish
   G risk
   H attempt
   J decision

3. Russian sailor Alexei Korkin is another person who might still be alive if he had **heeded** a premonition.
   A ignored
   B given
   C told someone
   D paid attention to

4. That same day, Mary Hennessy also sensed **impending** doom. She dreamed of many schoolchildren . . . . Something dreadful was happening to them.
   F approaching
   G terrible
   H landslide
   J tricky

5. Each one by itself made no sense. But taken together, they foretold the future. And they foretold it with frightening **clarity**.
   A inaccuracy
   B terror
   C style
   D clearness

6. So he looked for stories that could be **verified**. For instance, Carolyn Miller had told her friends about her vision the day before the tragedy. So it was clear that she was telling the truth.
   F repeated
   G proven to be true
   H written down
   J told by other people

PUT WORDS IN CONTEXT For each blank, choose one of the underlined words from this page that best completes the meaning of the paragraph.

A premonition is a feeling or a

_____. Usually, premonitions are

about _____ disaster. It's hard to

know when to pay attention to a premonition, but there

are a lot of people who might have avoided their own

deaths if they had _____ their

own feelings about what might happen. On the other

hand, people may have a bad feeling about something,

when there is no actual _____.

MULTIPLE MEANINGS Many words are spelled alike but have different meanings. You can determine the meaning of the word by seeing how the word is used in the sentence.

Read the definitions of each word. On the line, write the meaning of the underlined word as it is used in the sentence.

> **sail:** **1.** to move or proceed easily
> **2.** to begin a water voyage

1. **The ship was supposed to <u>sail</u> with Mrs. Straub on board.**

_____

2. **Ellen hoped to <u>sail</u> through her social studies test.**

_____

> **leaves:** **1.** more than one leaf
> **2.** goes away from

3. **The *General Slocum* <u>leaves</u> the shore and bursts into flames.**

_____

4. **Once ignited, very dry <u>leaves</u> can cause a forest fire.**

_____

> **ground:** **1.** the surface of the earth **2.** to keep from taking part in usual activities **3.** a basis for belief, action, or argument **4.** an object that makes an electrical connection with the earth

5. **Lindsay Wagner was on the <u>ground</u> when the plane took off.**

_____

6. **Jon's mom told him she would <u>ground</u> him if he came home late again.**

_____

> **bright:** **1.** intelligent or clever **2.** shining or glowing **3.** lively or cheerful **4.** promising

7. **A man in northwest England dreamed of seven letters surrounded by <u>bright</u> lights.**

_____

8. **The accident prevented hundreds of children from realizing a <u>bright</u> future.**

_____

> **watch:** **1.** to keep guard **2.** to observe **3.** a timepiece worn on the wrist **4.** a period of duty

9. **Carolyn Miller turned on the TV to <u>watch</u> news reports about Aberfan.**

_____

10. **It was 9:15 in the morning when the man in Aberfan looked at his <u>watch</u>.**

_____

PRACTICE SUMMARIZING As you now know, a summary retells the main points of a story. Summaries do not attempt to recount every detail. The reason summaries are useful is that they are always shorter than the original piece. For example, if you look up the TV guide in the newspaper, there is often a summary of what a show is about. A sentence is usually enough to summarize a half-hour program.

Practice writing one-sentence summaries of these TV programs about disasters. Use only one sentence. You decide what the show will be about based on the title. The first one is done for you.

SUMMARIZE THE STORIES In the space provided, write a one-paragraph summary of each of the selections. Be sure to include only the main points from each selection.

"They Saw It Coming"

_____
_____
_____
_____
_____
_____
_____

"A School Wiped Out"

_____
_____
_____
_____
_____
_____
_____

TV Program and One-sentence Summary
1. "Heroes of Forest Fires"
Reporter Susan Giles interviews firefighters who are trying to save the homes of people living in areas threatened by forest fires.
2. "Earthquake Rocks California"
3. "Hurricane Season Begins"
4. "Terror Warnings"

DRAW CONCLUSIONS You draw conclusions every day. You make judgments based on the information available to you. If you see a traffic jam when you get onto the highway, you may conclude that there is construction work or an accident. You may take an alternate route, or you may stay on the highway, depending on how much time you have. In big and little ways, you draw your own conclusions all the time. Read the following paragraph about premonitions and then choose the best answer to each question.

[1] Heeding a premonition could save your life. [2] No one is sure why premonitions occur, but they can be helpful warnings. [3] Some people think that premonitions are created by our own natural fears. [4] Even if they are, there could be serious consequences if you ignore premonitions. [5] If you think you've had a premonition about something, you have to decide whether to pay attention to it or not. [6] If you decide to ignore it, you may be risking more than you think.

1. **Which conclusion can you draw based on the paragraph above?**

   A Ignoring a premonition could be dangerous.

   B Everyone has premonitions sometimes.

   C Premonitions are caused by fear.

   D Premonitions only happen to people who believe in them.

2. **Which sentence from the paragraph explains the choice each person has to make?**

   F Sentence 2

   G Sentence 3

   H Sentence 4

   J Sentence 5

JUDGE THE EVIDENCE When you draw conclusions, you have to weigh the evidence. Choose the best answer.

1. **Which statement best supports the conclusion that Carolyn Miller's premonition had been real?**

   A Carolyn saw an "avalanche of coal" flowing down the mountain.

   B Carolyn lived in England where the disaster happened.

   C Carolyn told her friends about her vision before the disaster happened.

   D Carolyn was an honest woman.

2. **Which statement best supports the conclusion that the Aberfan schoolhouse accident was unavoidable?**

   F Many people had premonitions about the accident.

   G The children have to go to school every day, so they would have been there no matter what.

   H Even if you have a premonition, you can't avoid accidents.

   J None of the premonitions about the disaster made sense by themselves.

YOUR OWN CONCLUSION Do you think premonitions are real? Would you pay attention to one? Would you tell someone else about it? State your conclusions and support them with examples from both stories.

_____

_____

_____

_____

_____

_____

"Drive Toward Slidell!"

Rosemarie Kerr saw things that nobody else saw. Sometimes she saw the future. Sometimes she saw the past. Sometimes she saw things as they were happening. Rosemarie discovered her psychic ability when she was four years old. She dreamed of a house going up in flames. A few weeks later, a man across the street locked his wife and child in the bathroom and set fire to his house. Rosemarie realized that her terrible dream had come true.

By 1987, Rosemarie was no longer a little girl. She was a grown woman. She had moved away from her childhood home in New York and now lived in Cypress, California. But one thing hadn't changed. Her psychic powers were as strong as ever.

On June 11 of that year, Rosemarie got a call from Elise McGinley. Elise's brother, André Daigle, had been missing for two days. Elise and her family were frantic. Elise hoped Rosemarie could help.

Elise lived in California but André lived far away—in the town of Metaire, Louisiana. He had last been seen leaving a bar with a woman he met there. Rosemarie listened to Elise talk. She said she would do what she could. She asked Elise to bring her a picture of André and a map of Louisiana.

On June 13, Elise went to Rosemarie's house. Rosemarie took the picture of André and held it in her hands. She closed her eyes. Suddenly her head began to hurt. She told Elise this feeling came from André. She could feel great pain in his head. Near him she saw a black vehicle and a man with long, blond hair.

Moving to the map, Rosemarie closed her eyes again and ran her fingers over the map. She told Elise she saw water all around André. She also saw a bridge and a railroad track. She said the number "7" was important somehow. Then her fingers stopped moving. Her eyes popped open and she pointed to a town 30 miles from Metaire. It was called Slidell.

"Go there!" she cried. "Go there, quickly!"

Rosemarie insisted that Elise call her family right away. "Tell them to drive toward Slidell," she urged.

Elise did as Rosemarie instructed. It was late back in Louisiana. But Elise told her family not to wait. Rosemarie said they must go right away. The Daigle family was skeptical, but somehow they felt they could not ignore Rosemarie's command.

A group of family members climbed into a car and took off for Slidell. Mile after mile they drove, not sure what they were looking for. Then, a few miles from Slidell, they spotted it: André's truck. It was just ahead of them on I-10. They knew it was his vehicle because they could see a familiar scratch mark on the side. Pulling closer, they saw two men inside. Neither one was André. But one had long blond hair, just as Rosemarie had said.

As the family followed the truck, it turned into a high-speed chase. Luckily, a policeman joined the chase and helped corner the black truck. The two men inside, Charles Gervais and Michael Phillips, gave themselves up. The next day, these two men confessed to killing André Daigle.

Over time, the full story came out. The killers didn't know André. They had just been looking for someone to kill. They had asked a woman named Thelma Horne to help them pick a victim. On June 7, Thelma chose the bar where André happened to be. She asked him for a ride home. Once Thelma got André alone, Gervais and Phillips appeared. They hit André again and again on the head with a hammer. After eleven blows, he was still alive, so they strangled him.

Gervais told the police where they had dumped the body. It was in the Manchac swamp. As Rosemarie had suggested, a railroad track ran to the east of the swamp and there was a bridge nearby. The nearest interstate exit was number 7—the number Rosemarie had said would prove important.

For many, the story of André Daigle is compelling proof of Rosemarie Kerr's psychic powers. After all, she had no way of knowing that André drove a black truck. She couldn't have known that one of the killers had long, blond hair. She correctly saw water around the body. She also saw railroad tracks, a bridge, and the number "7." She somehow knew that André had experienced terrible head pain before he died. And she sent the family on a 30-mile drive in the middle of the night—a drive that led directly to the killers.

Skeptics brush these points aside. They say Rosemarie simply made good guesses. After all, Louisiana is a swampy state. So a killer would likely dump a body in some form of water. It was logical that there would be a bridge nearby and perhaps also a railroad track. Skeptics also point out that many killers hit their victims on the head and that "7" is a common number. Lots of people have long, blond hair. Lots of people drive black vehicles. As for Rosemarie's command to drive to Slidell, well, skeptics write that off as pure luck. They have no choice. There is no other way to explain it, except to admit that Rosemarie Kerr did indeed see things that no one else could see.

If you have been timed while reading this article, enter your reading time below. Then turn to the Words-per-Minute Table on page 120 and look up your reading speed (words per minute). Enter your reading speed on the graph on page 121.

Reading Time: Selection 1

_____ : _____
MINUTES   SECONDS

UNDERSTANDING IDEAS Circle the letter of the best answer.

1. **Which statement best describes Rosemarie Kerr's psychic ability?**

   A She saw the past, present, and future.

   B Her terrible dreams always came true.

   C She moved from New York to California.

   D She was just four years old when she started.

2. **Why did Elise McGinley call Rosemarie for help?**

   F They were old friends.

   G She wanted to be a psychic.

   H Her brother was missing.

   J She had a terrible headache.

3. **Which of these images from the story was NOT related to André's case?**

1. bridge

2. railroad tracks

3. number

4. burning house

   A Image 1

   B Image 2

   C Image 3

   D Image 4

4. **Based on the story of André Daigle, the reader can conclude that**

   F Rosemarie is known for making good guesses

   G skeptics were correct in brushing the evidence aside

   H most people like to believe that a person can have psychic powers

   J Rosemarie has special powers that most other people do not have

SUMMARIZE For each blank, choose the word that best completes the meaning of the paragraph.

vehicle	map	psychic
driven	missing	picture

Rosemarie Kerr had _____

abilities. In 1987, she was able to help find a

_____ person. She held a

_____ of the missing person and

a _____ of Louisiana. Rosemarie

saw a black _____ and felt a

great pain in her head. André's truck was discovered

being _____ by two men who

confessed to killing André Daigle.

IF YOU WERE THERE If someone you loved were missing, would you consult a psychic? Why or why not? Write a brief paragraph explaining what you would do. Be sure to include examples from the story to support your response.

_____

_____

_____

_____

_____

_____

Looking for Norman Lewis

On March 24, 1994, Norman Lewis left his house in Williston, Florida. The 76-year-old man climbed into his Chevy truck and drove off. He didn't plan to be gone long. He didn't even take his wallet with him. But hours passed and Lewis did not return. Days went by. The police looked for him, but found nothing. On April 11, Williston Police Chief Olin Slaughter told a reporter, "It's like he fell off the edge of the earth."

For two years, no one could figure out what had happened to Norman Lewis. Then a police detective made an unusual suggestion. Why not bring in a psychic? The detective had heard a lecture by psychic Noreen Renier. He thought she sounded pretty good. Lewis' family was desperate. They felt they had nothing to lose. And so they agreed to pay Noreen Renier's $650 fee.

Renier lived far away in Orlando, Florida. She had never been to Williston. She had never met Norman Lewis or his family. But she agreed to try her "psychometry" on the case. Psychometry is the ability to get information just by touching an object. Psychometrists believe that every person has a unique energy field. When someone touches an object, he or she leaves traces of that energy field behind. The energy field can contain all kinds of information. It can

contain thoughts, images, and feelings. So by holding an object that belonged to Lewis, Renier thought she might be able to discover what had happened to him.

The police sent her Lewis' wallet and one of his shoes. When she sat down with these items, she began to describe things about Lewis' life. She said, for instance, that he was retired from the military. This was true. Renier "knew" so much about Norman Lewis that both the police and the Lewis family were impressed.

Then Renier began describing images. She seemed to be seeing exactly what had happened to Lewis back in March of 1994. Renier said she saw his truck veering off the road. It went over some sort of steep cliff. She said, "No one really knows what's down there because it's so hazardous and dangerous that people don't go down there."

Renier said Lewis' body "must be still somehow in the vehicle. I feel the metal very, very strongly." She said the vehicle was "swallowed up" by water. This water was "in something like a pit." There were a lot of rocks around. There was also a railroad track. Finally, Renier gave the police two numbers: 45 and 21.

After hearing what Renier said, the Williston police debated what to do. There were several bodies of water near Norman Lewis' home. One was an old limestone quarry. This fit Renier's description of a dangerous pit with lots of rocks. The sides of the quarry were steep, forming the kind of cliff Renier mentioned. A lake now covered the quarry. This matched Renier's comment about the pit being filled with water. And there was one more thing. The road that ran alongside the quarry was state route 45—one of the numbers that Renier mentioned.

Not all the clues fit. Renier said there was a railroad track around. As far as the police knew, no train tracks ran through the quarry. Then there was the number "21." That didn't make any sense at all.

Still, police decided it was worth checking the quarry. They hired navy divers to come in. As the divers began their search, nearby workers dug something up. It was part of an old railroad track. So a track did indeed run through the area.

A few hours later, divers found what they were looking for. Sitting at the bottom of the quarry, under 20 feet of muddy water, was Norman Lewis' truck. His skeleton was still inside. Later the police realized that the truck had been found 2.1 miles from Lewis' home. That could explain why Renier saw the number "21."

Police Chief Slaughter gave Noreen Renier a lot of credit for solving the Norman Lewis case. "I don't think we ever would have found him without her help," Slaughter said.

Some people disagreed. A man named Gary P. Posner was not impressed. He believed anyone could have guessed that Lewis and his truck were at the bottom of a lake. In a report for *Tampa Bay Skeptics*, Posner wrote, "Where could they *possibly* be? In the middle of an extremely densely wooded area? In an abandoned building? (Either, perhaps, if only a body was missing. But a truck?) Only one possibility even comes to mind— submerged under water."

Posner pointed out that many days had passed between the time police first contacted Renier and when she sat down to do her psychometry reading. So she had plenty of time to research the details of Norman Lewis' life. She could have seen maps of Williston. She could have learned about the old quarry, state road 45, and even the railroad track. Renier said she would never do such a thing. But some people weren't so sure.

Renier was not surprised. "I understand the skeptics," she told one reporter. "Everyone should have some skepticism." Still, Renier maintained that her powers were real. "It's an ability that I've nurtured and developed," she declared. She also said, "I think a lot of people have psychic abilities, but they just never take the time to develop them."

If you have been timed while reading this article, enter your reading time below. Then turn to the Words-per-Minute Table on page 120 and look up your reading speed (words per minute). Enter your reading speed on the graph on page 121.

Reading Time: Selection 2

_____ : _____
MINUTES   SECONDS

UNDERSTANDING IDEAS
Circle the letter of the best answer.

1. Why was a psychic consulted in the case of Norman Lewis?

A Lewis did not take his wallet with him.

B A psychic convinced his family that she could find him.

C For two years no one could figure out what happened to him.

D The family thought that Noreen Renier's fee was reasonable.

2. How do psychometrists get information about a missing person?

F by doing careful research

G by interviewing the person's family

H by leaving traces of his or her energy field

J by touching objects that belong to the person

3. How did Noreen Renier impress the Lewis family and the police?

A She was able to describe things about Lewis' life.

B She said that Lewis had left behind traces of his energy field.

C She lived far away in Florida and had never been to Williston.

D She told them that she might be able to tell what happened to him.

4. Which statement explains why Gary P. Posner was skeptical of Renier's psychic abilities?

F The police were giving Renier a lot of credit for solving the Lewis case.

G Anyone who had done some research could have guessed where Lewis was.

H Renier declared that she had nurtured and developed her psychic abilities.

J Renier had spent a lot of time in Williston and knew Norman Lewis.

SUMMARIZE
For each blank, choose the word that best completes the meaning of the paragraph.

believed	shoes	truck	psycho-metrist
skeleton	disappeared	quarry	

Norman Lewis _____ from his home on March 24, 1994. He drove off in his _____ and never returned. For two years, police were stumped. Then Noreen Renier, a practicing _____, got involved. The family sent her one of Lewis' _____ and his wallet. Renier said that she _____ he was still in his truck somewhere. Divers found Lewis' _____ in his truck, in a _____, under 20 feet of water.

IF YOU WERE THERE
Imagine that you were a member of Lewis' family. What steps would you take to find him? Write a brief paragraph explaining what you might do. Be sure to include examples from the story to support your response.

_____

_____

_____

_____

_____

USE CONTEXT CLUES When you read, you may find a word whose meaning is unfamiliar to you. When that happens, you can look up the word's meaning in the dictionary. You can also find out what the word means by looking for context clues. These are words or sentences that come before or after the word. Context clues can be words with the same or opposite meanings as the unfamiliar word. They may also be an example or definition of the unfamiliar word.

Read each excerpt from the stories you just read. Circle the letter with the best meaning of the underlined word.

1. **Elise's brother, André Daigle, had been missing for two days. Elise and her family were frantic.**

   A a bit worried

   B somewhat concerned

   C very angry

   D wildly anxious

2. **Rosemarie said they must go right away. The Daigle family was skeptical, but somehow they felt they could not ignore Rosemarie's command.**

   F upset

   G doubtful

   H curious

   J relieved

3. **For many, the story of André Daigle is compelling proof of Rosemarie Kerr's psychic powers. After all, she had no way of knowing that André drove a black truck.**

   A weird

   B unusual

   C powerful

   D useless

4. **Renier said she saw his truck veering off the road. It went over some sort of steep cliff.**

   F turning sharply

   G stopping

   H climbing

   J spiraling

5. **"No one really knows what's down there because it's so hazardous and dangerous that people don't go down there."**

   A dark

   B steep

   C unsafe

   D rough

PUT WORDS INTO CONTEXT Complete the paragraph using the underlined words from the exercise on this page.

You may be _____ as to whether or not people actually have psychic powers. Sometimes, even people who don't believe in psychics will go to one if they are _____ enough. Worry can be a _____ reason to seek the help of a psychic.

USING EXACT WORDS You can make your writing come alive for the reader by using exact, or highly specific words. Exact words help to create vivid mental pictures in the mind of your reader. For example, which sentence gives you a better image? [1] The flowers were in bloom in the garden. [2] The bright purple violets spilled over onto the walkway. Sentence 2 gives you a specific mental picture because of the colorful adjectives, nouns, and verbs used in the sentence. In sentence 1, you aren't even sure what flowers to picture.

Read these sentences from the stories and choose the MOST exact word to replace the underlined word.

1. **Suddenly her head began to hurt.**
   A throb
   B spin
   C mistreat
   D swell

2. **It was late back in Louisiana.**
   F after dark
   G nighttime
   H around suppertime
   J almost midnight

3. **They hit André again and again on the head with a hammer.**
   A contacted
   B pounded
   C touched
   D rubbed

4. **Renier lived far away in Orlando, Florida.**
   F a good bit
   G some distance
   H several hundred miles
   J quite a few miles

5. **She could have seen maps of Williston.**
   A glanced at
   B studied
   C come across
   D found

ANALOGIES As you have seen in previous exercises, analogies show relationships and patterns between words. The relationships can be very different things, not just synonyms and antonyms. For example, *hat* is to *head* as *glove* is to *hand*. The first words (*hat* and *glove*) are meant to cover the second words (*head* and *hand*). For each blank, choose an underlined word from the exercise on this page to correctly complete the analogy. In most cases, you will only use one of the underlined words.

1. *Near* is to *close* as _____ is to *distant*.

2. *Slow* is to *fast* as _____ is to *on time*.

3. *Heard* is to *radio* as _____ is to *television*.

4. *Kick* is to *punt* as _____ is to *smack*.

5. *Cry* is to *tears* as _____ is to *pain*.

ORGANIZE THE FACTS There are several different ways to organize your writing. In stories like the ones you just read, the sequence, or order, of the events is very important. In the chart below, fill in the next event in the order that it happened. Then complete the chart for "Looking for Norman Lewis."

"Drive Toward Slidell!"

1. On June 11, Elise McGinley tells Rosemarie that her brother André has been missing for two days and asks for help.

2. On June 13, Elise takes a picture of André to Rosemarie's house.

3. Rosemarie tells Elise that her family must drive to Slidell.

4.

5. The men confess that they beat and strangled André.

"Looking for Norman Lewis"

1. March 24, 1994, Norman Lewis leaves his house in Williston, Florida, and never returns.

2.

3.

4.

5.

PUT DETAILS IN SEQUENCE
Choose the best answer for each question.

1. **When did the following happen? Where should it be in the sequence chart about "Drive Toward Slidell"?**

   Rosemarie Kerr felt a terrible pain in her head.

   A before 1
   B between 1 and 2
   C between 2 and 3
   D between 3 and 4

2. **In the chart about "Looking for Norman Lewis," where would you place the information about the railroad track being discovered by workers?**
   F at the beginning of the list
   G in the middle of the list
   H toward the end of the list
   J nowhere on the chart

MAKE PREDICTIONS You can make predictions, or educated guesses, based on what you already know. For example, you know that there is a traffic jam on the main highway every day between five and six o'clock in the evening. Based on this knowledge, you can reasonably predict that tomorrow's traffic will be the same.

Read this passage, and answer the following questions based on what you know after reading the stories.

Vanished Without a Trace

Kim Green, a good friend of Elise McGinley, was awakened one morning by a phone call. It was her husband's boss calling to say that Kim's husband Peter had not shown up for work that morning. Alarmed, Kim immediately began calling Peter's cell phone. She got no answer, so she called local hospitals asking if a man named Peter Green had been admitted. She came up with nothing and decided to call the police. They told her that a person must be missing for 24 hours before they can file a report, but that they would be on the lookout for Peter's car.

---

1. **What do you predict Kim will do next?**

   A dial Peter's cell phone again

   B call her friend Elise McGinley

   C go to hospitals in nearby towns

   D wait 24 hours and call the police again

2. **When Elise finds out about Peter's disappearance, what do you predict she will do to help?**

   F tell Kim to call the police

   G hope that Kim's husband is OK

   H contact psychic Rosemarie Kerr

   J contact other members of Kim's family

3. **Predict what a skeptic from the local paper would NOT say to Kim.**

   A Remain calm.

   B Call the police.

   C Get in touch with a psychic.

   D Call all of Peter's friends.

JUDGE THE BASIS OF A PREDICTION For predictions to be reasonably accurate, they must be based on what you know as factual information. Choose the best answer.

1. **Which statement helps you predict that Rosemarie Kerr might help find Kim's husband?**

   A Rosemarie helped find Elise's brother.

   B Rosemarie has been a psychic for a long time.

   C She helped the police find missing people.

   D She proved to skeptics that her powers were real.

2. **Which statement helps you predict that a skeptic would not tell Kim to ask Rosemarie Kerr for help?**

   F Rosemarie has not helped skeptics find missing people.

   G Skeptics believe that Rosemarie simply made good guesses.

   H Rosemarie lives too far away from where Peter disappeared.

   J Skeptics need more proof that Rosemarie had special powers.

PREDICT WHAT YOU WOULD DO Write a brief paragraph explaining what you would do if a friend or family member were missing. Use examples from the stories you just read to explain your decisions.

_____

_____

_____

_____

_____

_____

The Great Edgar Cayce

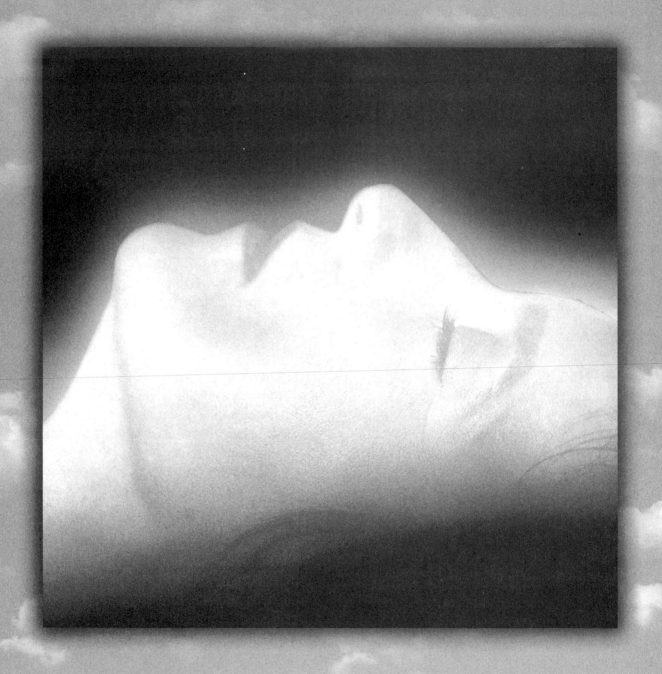

Aime Dietrich was two years old when she came down with the flu. The illness had a terrible effect on her. It damaged her body and destroyed her personality. For the next three years, Aime's mind seemed nearly blank. Her body shook and trembled. The Dietrich family feared their little girl had no future. Then, in 1902, a man named Edgar Cayce stepped into their lives. Could this poorly educated farmboy save Aime?

The Dietrichs believed he could. Cayce seemed to have special powers. He hadn't gone to college. He hadn't even finished high school. Yet people said he could find cures in cases doctors thought were hopeless.

Cayce had discovered his gift in 1899 at the age of 21. It happened after he lost his voice. He became unable to speak above a whisper. Doctors examined him but offered no solution. The condition seemed permanent. Then Cayce fell into some sort of trance. In this altered state, he spoke in a loud, clear voice. He told his astonished family that more blood needed to flow to his throat. As he said this, the blood vessels in his neck apparently responded and his throat turned hot and red. When he awoke, he was cured.

After that, friends began coming to Cayce with their medical problems.

Cayce would lie down, close his eyes, and place his hands over his stomach. Then he would fall into a sleep-like trance. In an eloquent voice, he would explain what was wrong with the person, and what the treatment should be. It turned out that the person didn't even have to be in the room. Cayce could do a "reading" based simply on someone's name and address. He could diagnose and prescribe treatments from miles away.

When Cayce did a reading for Aime Dietrich, he made a surprising diagnosis. Aime's troubles sprang not from the flu, but from a fall she had taken days before getting sick. Cayce declared that Aime's back had been injured. She could recover if her spine was moved in certain specific ways.

The Dietrich family followed Cayce's directions. And Aime did indeed begin to improve. Soon she recognized a favorite doll. Then she recognized her parents. Within three months, she had completely recovered.

As a result of such cases, Cayce's fame grew. He became known as the "Sleeping Prophet." When he came out of a trance, he had no idea what he had said. It was as if he had been asleep the whole time. Yet during his readings, he spoke in sophisticated terms. He showed detailed knowledge of the human body. He made medical references that only doctors understood. This was amazing because Cayce had never been to medical school. Cayce's supporters claimed he could do other amazing things as well. They said he could absorb the contents of a book just by sleeping on it. They said he could cure "incurable" diseases.

In 1911, Cayce's wife Gertrude became desperately ill. Doctors said she had tuberculosis, a very serious lung disease. Cayce went into a trance to find a cure. He said she should take some medicine. She should also breathe in fumes from apple brandy stored in a charred oak keg. Gertrude did this. When she recovered a few months later, Cayce got credit for saving her life.

People from around the country flooded Edgar Cayce with requests for help. By the time Cayce died in 1945, he had given more than 14,000 readings. His secretary, Gladys Davis, wrote down what he said during all his trances. These records can be found at Edgar Cayce's Association for Research and Enlightenment.

People today still wonder what special powers—if any—Cayce really had. His knowledge of medicine can be partly explained by the fact that he read a lot. He educated himself about the body and its weaknesses. And some of his treatment plans succeeded because they made good sense. He was ahead of his time in understanding the importance of diet, exercise, and relaxation. But often Cayce's instructions were just plain bizarre. He recommended "bedbug juice" for a blood problem. For breast cancer, he suggested rubbing the skin with "the raw side of a freshly skinned

rabbit, still warm with blood." It is hard to believe that these "cures" had any value at all.

In fact, the records show many cases where Edgar Cayce's suggestions did not work. Some of these cases are heartbreaking. One man begged Cayce to cure his severely retarded daughter. A mother asked Cayce to end her son's blindness. A woman hoped her paralyzed daughter might walk again. These people and thousands like them believed in Cayce's ability to work miracles. They did their best to follow whatever advice he gave them. When the treatments didn't work, some people blamed themselves. They figured they had not followed Cayce's instructions precisely enough. Others refused to see that the treatments weren't working.

Then there are cases like Aime Dietrich's. How did Cayce know the cure for this little girl? Was it a miracle or a lucky guess? Was her recovery just a coincidence that had nothing to do with Cayce's treatment? Was the whole story a lie or exaggeration? To this day, people can't agree on the answers.

If you have been timed while reading this article, enter your reading time below. Then turn to the Words-per-Minute Table on page 120 and look up your reading speed (words per minute). Enter your reading speed on the graph on page 121.

Reading Time: Selection 1

_____ : _____
MINUTES   SECONDS

UNDERSTANDING IDEAS Circle the letter of the best answer.

1. **How did Edgar Cayce discover his special gift?**

   A Doctors examined him.

   B He visited the Dietrich family.

   C He cured his inability to speak while in a trance.

   D Friends were coming to him with their medical problems.

2. **What did Cayce say was the cause of Aime Dietrich's illness?**

   F the flu

   G pnuemonia

   H appendicitis

   J a back injury

3. **Which statement expresses doubt about Cayce's special powers?**

   A Thousands of people believed in Cayce's ability to work miracles

   B When he came out of a trance, he had no idea what he had said.

   C His medical knowledge can be partly explained by the fact that he read a lot.

   D Records of his treatments can be found at the Association for Research and Enlightenment.

4. **Based on the examples of Cayce's treatments, which statement can you infer?**

   F It is hard to believe that any of Cayce's cures had any value at all.

   G Although he never went to medical school, Cayce was a true doctor.

   H Some of Cayce's treatments worked because they made good sense and were based on knowledge of the body and its weaknesses.

   J Cayce's supporters claimed he could do amazing things, such as absorbing the contents of a book just by sleeping on it.

SUMMARIZE For each blank, choose the word that best completes the meaning of the paragraph.

months	afraid	recover	
readings	trance	treatment	sought

The Dietrich family was _____

that their daughter Aime would never

_____ from her strange illness. They

_____ the help of a man named Edgar

Cayce. Aime recovered in three _____,

apparently as a result of Cayce's advice. Cayce did

_____ for people by going into a

sleep-like _____. Then he would

explain what was wrong with the person and what the

_____ should be.

IF YOU WERE THERE Write a brief paragraph explaining what you would have done if you were one of Aime Dietrich's parents. Would you have gone to Cayce? Be sure to include examples from the story in your response.

_____

_____

_____

_____

_____

Psychic Surgery

an McKee was in pain. He was having terrible headaches. He was also having bad nosebleeds. He couldn't stand it. He needed relief. So in 1980, Dan went to Baguio City, Philippines. There he sought out a man named Marcelino. This man promised to help him. Marcelino told Dan he needed surgery. But it wouldn't be ordinary surgery. It would be done without painkillers. There would be no knife, no stitches, no scar, and no pain. In short, Marcelino would perform "psychic surgery."

Marcelino had Dan lie down on a hard wooden table. Then Marcelino began to move his hands over Dan's bare chest. With one hand, he made a cutting motion. Although Dan felt no pain, blood began to ooze over his chest. Marcelino's fingers seemed to disappear down into Dan's body. Marcelino moved his hands a bit. Then he pulled out a bloody lump of tissue.

A few seconds later, Marcelino was finished. An assistant wiped up the blood. Dan sat up. He looked at his chest. There was no scar at all. Then he realized his headache was gone. His nose was no longer bleeding. He felt wonderful. His body seemed healthy. And his mind felt peaceful.

Marcelino smiled at him. He said there had been a blood clot blocking a vein in Dan's chest. Marcelino had removed the blood clot, and so Dan was cured. Since that day, Dan has been free from headaches. He hasn't had any more nosebleeds, either.

Stories like Dan McKee's are common among people who believe in psychic surgery. True believers say psychic surgeons can fix all sorts of problems. They can get rid of back pain. They can make people walk again. They can even cure cancer.

Psychic surgery has its roots in the Philippines. There, people traditionally believed that evil spirits caused sickness. Sick people went to healers who often appeared to pull objects out of their patients' bodies. Sometimes the object was a coin. Sometimes it was a chicken's foot. In any case, healers said that evil spirits had put the object in the patient's body. Once the object was removed, the patient was "cured."

In the 1960s, Philippine healers began performing their magic tricks on Americans. They didn't use the term "evil spirits." Instead, healers offered to remove "negative energy" from the patient's body. They claimed removing it would cure all sorts of problems. They also offered to take out blood clots, tumors, and diseased tissue. A surprising number of people took them seriously. Soon, psychic surgeons had many followers in America.

Actress Shirley MacLaine was one follower. She met psychic surgeon Alex Orbito in Las Vegas. There he removed "negative energy clots" from her body. MacLaine was dazzled by Orbito's work. She invited him back to her California home. There, about a hundred of her friends lined up to have Orbito perform psychic surgery on them. The man became an instant celebrity.

In 1973, Dr. William A. Nolen went to the Philippines. Nolen was a real surgeon. He wanted to find out exactly what healers like Orbito were doing. He hoped to gain important insights into the mind and body. That same year, Donald and Carol Wright also traveled to the Philippines. The Wrights believed strongly in psychic surgery. They wanted to assist healers. But in the end, both Nolen and the Wrights were disappointed. They came to the same conclusions. The healers were faking the whole thing.

The Wrights discovered that healers wrapped bits of animal tissue in wads of cotton. They hid a wad under their belt or beneath their collar. As the "surgery" began, they slipped it into their hand. They pushed down on the patient's skin and made a cutting motion. At the same time, they squeezed the wad of cotton. And so, indeed, blood would begin to ooze. But it was animal blood, not the patient's blood. Often an assistant would "wipe the blood away." But he or she was really adding water to make a bigger pool of blood. By bending their fingers in the blood, healers made it look like their hands were deep inside the patient's body. Then they would hold up the wad of cotton. They told patients it was a "blood clot" or a "negative energy clot" or even a "tumor."

Nolen found the same thing. He watched healers pull out all sorts of things from wads of bloody cotton. A "tumor" turned out to be a clump of fat. A "kidney stone" was really just a lump of sugar.

Today most real doctors agree that psychic surgery is a hoax. But people like Dan McKee still say psychic surgery cured them. Investigator George Nava True II thinks he knows why. After the "surgery," patients relax. They believe they are cured. They stop worrying. So if their pain was caused by stress, the pain does indeed go away.

The problem, of course, is that not all problems are caused by stress. In 1984, actor Andy Kaufman had lung cancer. He went to Philippine healer Ramon "Jun" Labo Jr. who performed psychic surgery on him. Labo appeared to pull a bloody mass out of Kaufman's chest. He told the actor he had removed all the cancer. Kaufman believed him. But two months later, Kaufman died. The cause of death? Lung cancer.

If you have been timed while reading this article, enter your reading time below. Then turn to the Words-per-Minute Table on page 120 and look up your reading speed (words per minute). Enter your reading speed on the graph on page 121.

Reading Time: Selection 2

———— : ————
MINUTES   SECONDS

UNDERSTANDING IDEAS Circle the letter of the best answer.

1. Why did Dan McKee seek the help of a psychic surgeon?

A He was afraid of surgery.

B He had neck and back pain.

C He had headaches and nosebleeds.

D He didn't want stitches or scars on him.

2. What did Marcelino say was wrong with McKee?

F His body seemed healthy.

G He said he had a blood clot.

H His head needed surgery.

J He said that nosebleeds are common.

3. Psychic surgery is originally based on which belief?

A Healers are magicians.

B Evil spirits cause sickness.

C Psychic surgeons are real doctors.

D Americans like alternative healers.

4. Which conclusion did Dr. William A. Nolen reach after observing psychic surgery in the Philippines?

F Some people could be helped by psychic surgery.

G The entire surgery was being faked.

H Anyone who believed in the surgery could be cured.

J Healers could remove negative energy from a patient.

SUMMARIZE For each blank, choose the word that best completes the meaning of the paragraph.

cured	perform	surgeon
surgery	incision	hoax

Psychic _____ had its roots in

the Philippines. Surgeons could reportedly

_____ surgery without

making an _____. A psychic

_____ in the Philippines

reportedly performed such a surgery on a man named

Dan McKee. Dan believed that the man named Marcelino

_____ him. Most doctors

today believe that psychic surgery is a

_____.

IF YOU WERE THERE Imagine that you are either Donald or Carol Wright and that you have traveled a long way to assist psychic healers. What were some of your observations? Be sure to include examples from the story to support your response.

_____

_____

_____

_____

_____

_____

USE CONTEXT CLUES When you read, you may find a word whose meaning is unfamiliar to you. When that happens, you can look up the word's meaning in the dictionary. You can also find out what the word means by looking for context clues. These are words or sentences that come before or after the word. Context clues can be words with the same or opposite meanings as the unfamiliar word. They may also be an example or definition of the unfamiliar word.

Read each excerpt from the stories you just read. Circle the letter with the best meaning of the underlined word.

1. In this altered state, he spoke in a loud, clear voice. He told his astonished family that more blood needed to flow to his throat.

   A shocked

   B large

   C immediate

   D nervous

2. When Cayce did a reading for Aime Dietrich, he made a suprising diagnosis. Aime's troubles sprang not from the flu, but from a fall she had taken days before getting sick.

   F cure

   G improvement

   H medical observation

   J recovery

3. Yet during his readings, he spoke in sophisticated terms. He showed detailed knowledge of the human body. He made medical references that only doctors understood.

   A low-level

   B complex

   C broad

   D interesting

4. A "tumor" turned out to be a clump of fat. A "kidney stone" was really just a lump of sugar. Today most real doctors agree that psychic surgery is a hoax.

   F cure

   G help

   H fraud

   J medication

5. They pushed down on the patient's skin and made a cutting motion. At the same time, they squeezed the wad of cotton. And so, indeed, blood would begin to ooze.

   A seep out

   B thicken

   C flood

   D clot

PUT WORDS INTO CONTEXT Complete the paragraph using the underlined words from the exercise on this page.

Around the turn of the century, Edgar Cayce

_____ people with his ability

to diagnose medical problems. Cayce was not

a doctor, but when he spoke in a trance,

he would make a _____ using

_____ medical language.

Many people think psychic surgery is a

_____, but Cayce had many

followers who believed in his abilities.

SIMILES AND METAPHORS Writers use similes and metaphors to make their writing more vivid. Similes and metaphors are comparisons between words. Similes are easy to spot because they are preceded by the words *like* or *as*. Here's an example: *She was as graceful as a bird.* Here's another simile: *Jack is tall like an oak tree.* Metaphors are a little different because the comparisons do not use the words *like* or *as*. Here's an example of a metaphor: *Russell was a lion in the courtroom.* The sentence means that Russell is strong and aggressive. Another metaphor: *Baseball is life.* The sentence simply means that baseball is very important to whoever made that statement.

Read the following sentences. Decide whether the comparison is a simile or metaphor. Write S for simile or M for metaphor in the blank on the left.

_____ **1.** To the Dietrichs, Cayce was an angel from heaven.

_____ **2.** When Edgar Cayce was in a trance-like state, he was like a different person.

_____ **3.** For people who believed Cayce cured them, he was as good as a medical doctor.

_____ **4.** Long ago, people believed that sickness was an evil spirit.

_____ **5.** To Shirley MacLaine, Orbito was a dazzling miracle maker.

WHAT'S THE COMPARISON? Read the following sentences. In the space provided, write what two things are being compared.

1. Dan McKee's headaches were like sledgehammers.

_____

2. Marcelino was a magician who cured Dan of both his headaches and nosebleeds.

_____

3. Alex Orbito's career took off like a rocket after Shirley MacLaine brought a hundred of her friends to have psychic surgery.

_____

4. Dr. William Nolen and Donald and Carol Wright found the psychic surgeons they visited to be as phony as three-dollar bills.

_____

5. After having psychic surgery, Dan McKee thought he was as healthy as a newborn baby.

_____

ORGANIZE IDEAS The main ideas in a story are the main topics that are discussed. The specific details are the facts that clarify or support the main ideas. Fill in the charts by using the items listed at the right. If the bulleted item is a main idea from the story, write it in the row marked "Main Idea." If the item is a detail that supports the main idea, write it in a row marked "Detail."

"The Great Edgar Cayce"
Main Idea:
Detail:
Detail:
Detail:
Detail:

"Psychic Surgery"
Main Idea:
Detail:
Detail:
Detail:
Detail:

- He went into a trance-like state to diagnose people's illnesses.

- Like Dr. Nolen, most real doctors now believe that psychic surgery is a hoax.

- Edgar Cayce has been credited with saving the lives of many people.

- Dr. Nolen traveled to observe the surgeons doing their work.

- Marcelino said that a blood clot was causing Dan McKee's problems.

- By the time he died, he had given over 14,000 readings.

- Aime Dietrich was sick for nearly three years before being cured.

- Psychic surgeons say they can cure problems without a knife or pain.

- Actor Andy Kaufman died of lung cancer, in spite of his visit to a Philippine healer.

- He had an excellent knowledge of the body and how it worked.

SUPPORT THE MAIN IDEA Write a paragraph about miracle healers. State the main idea in the first sentence. Then use details from both stories to support your main idea.

_____

_____

_____

_____

_____

_____

MAKE INFERENCES Inferences are what the reader learns from what the writer has written. When you make an inference, you consider the evidence you've read and then decide what the message is. Circle the letter of the best answer.

1. **What can the reader infer from these sentences?**

   > Cayce seemed to have special powers. He hadn't gone to college or finished high school. Yet people said he could find cures in cases doctors thought were hopeless.

   A Doctors don't typically label a case as hopeless.

   B The writer doesn't believe Cayce is unusual.

   C Only people who have gone to college have special powers.

   D The writer expects someone with "special powers" to be well-educated.

2. **What can the reader infer from this sentence?**

   > As he [Cayce] said this, the blood vessels in his neck apparently responded and his throat turned hot and red.

   F Cayce's throat did not turn hot and red.

   G There is no doubt that Cayce's neck responded.

   H The writer doubts whether Cayce's body really responded.

   J The writer hopes that Cayce's body does not turn hot and red.

APPLY WHAT YOU KNOW

1. **Read the following sentence. Why do you think the author put the phrase below in quotes?**

   > In short, Marcelino would perform "psychic surgery."

   A to create a sense of uncertainty

   B to give credit to Marcelino

   C to show how psychic surgery is a miracle

   D to explain psychic surgery

2. **By saying that "a surprising number of people took them [psychic surgeons] seriously," the author probably wanted to**

   F tell readers that psychic healers are good doctors

   G show that believing in a psychic surgeon is foolish

   H make the psychic healing stories sound more believable

   J show amazement that more people didn't take them seriously

JUDGE THE EVIDENCE Based on what you have read from both stories, do you believe miracle healers are real, or do you think they are deceiving people? Write a brief paragraph stating what you believe. Support your opinion with evidence from the stories.

_____

_____

_____

_____

_____

_____

Is Hypnosis Dangerous?

It was Christopher Gates' birthday, and his girlfriend wanted to do something special for him. So she got tickets to a show at a theatre in High Wycombe, England. The show featured a well-known hypnotist named Paul McKenna. Thirty-four-year-old Chris seemed to enjoy the performance. He even volunteered to go up on stage and be hypnotized. But after the evening ended, things started to go wrong. First Chris got a terrible headache. Then he began to hear voices in his head. Nine days after the show, he was admitted to a psychiatric hospital. Chris hadn't had problems before the show. So he and his girlfriend began to wonder: did the hypnosis cause his mental illness?

That question came before a judge in 1998 when Chris sued Paul McKenna. Chris claimed that the hypnosis had changed him forever. He wanted the hypnotist to pay $700,000 for the damage done.

According to Chris, he hadn't wanted to participate in the show in the first place. He said Paul McKenna had somehow hypnotized him without his permission at the very beginning of the evening, when Chris was still in his seat. So when McKenna asked for volunteers, Chris really didn't have a choice. "It was just a compulsion," said Chris, "and I

shot out of my chair and went up on the stage. I was the first there."

During McKenna's two-hour show, a hypnotized Chris entertained the audience. When McKenna suggested that Chris was a ballet dancer, Chris pranced across the stage. When McKenna told Chris he was Mick Jaggar, Chris began acting like the famous rock star. There were other volunteers up on the stage that night, but everyone agreed that Chris was the star of the show.

While he was hypnotized, Chris seemed willing to believe anything McKenna told him. He believed he had won a million dollars. He believed he was an interpreter for aliens. He thought he was walking on the moon. He became afraid of a broom and tried to use a shoe as a telephone. He even believed he was wearing special glasses that let him see through people's clothes.

From Paul McKenna's point of view, this was all just good entertainment. "My show is a fun show," McKenna told Mr. Justice Toulson, the High Court judge. McKenna said people were free to participate or not—it was their choice. McKenna said he watched for signs of distress in his volunteers. If any of them seemed upset, he offered them the chance to stop. "And when I speak to somebody as they leave, I remind them that they are now completely back to normal."

Chris Gates, however, didn't return to normal. When the show ended, Chris didn't remember anything he had done on stage. But that night he had trouble sleeping. And he developed a terrible headache. "My mind was buzzing," he said. "It was ringing in my head."

The next day, Chris went to work, but his boss noticed something wrong. Chris' personality seemed different. He giggled and cried his way through a work meeting. And he became angry over little things.

Over the next few days, Chris' girlfriend noticed these changes, too. When they went out, she said, Chris began "laughing hysterically, in an exaggerated way." She said it was "totally inappropriate." He "laughed hysterically at everything and anything." When told he might lose his job, he burst into a fit of giggles. At the same time, Chris became afraid to go to sleep at night. He refused to take a shower or go upstairs. He felt he was being watched. He heard voices. He was convinced that something inside his head was destroying him.

Nine days after participating in Paul McKenna's show, Chris entered a psychiatric hospital. He was diagnosed with schizophrenia. People with this disorder can't tell what is real and what is fantasy.

Chris had been perfectly healthy before the show. He had shown no signs of schizophrenia or any other disorder. His family had no history of mental illness. So he believed hypnosis must have caused his problems. Chris' therapist, Derek Crussell, agreed. Mr. Crussell said he was "quite sure"

that Chris' illness had been "triggered" by the hypnosis.

Paul McKenna disagreed. McKenna maintained that hypnosis was "perfectly safe." He said, "it works only if the person wants it to." For McKenna, hypnosis was not "some magic power." It couldn't turn a healthy person into a sick one.

For two weeks, the judge listened to both sides of the case. In the end, he agreed with Paul McKenna. The judge said he understood why Chris blamed hypnosis for his problems. But the judge saw no link between hypnosis and schizophrenia. It was just a coincidence that Chris' illness appeared so soon after McKenna's show.

Paul McKenna was delighted by the ruling. He said he felt "great sympathy" for Chris, but he believed the verdict "has proved conclusively that hypnosis was not and could not have been the cause of his schizophrenia."

Chris' lawyer was not so sure. "The judge has found that Chris' illness was not triggered by the hypnosis," the lawyer pointed out, "but he did not find that stage hypnosis is safe."

If you have been timed while reading this article, enter your reading time below. Then turn to the Words-per-Minute Table on page 120 and look up your reading speed (words per minute). Enter your reading speed on the graph on page 121.

Reading Time: Selection 1

_____ : _____
MINUTES   SECONDS

UNDERSTANDING IDEAS Circle the letter of the best answer.

1. **Which of the following statements is FALSE?**

   A Chris volunteered to go up on stage.

   B Chris had a history of mental illness.

   C Chris began to hear voices in his head.

   D Chris seemed to enjoy McKenna's performance.

2. **Chris Gates believes that Paul McKenna's show**

   F caused his illness

   G was very entertaining

   H is harmless for healthy people

   J caused Gates' girlfriend to leave him

3. **What reason did the judge have for disagreeing with Chris Gates?**

   A He did not believe that Chris Gates was sick.

   B He had been entertained by Paul McKenna's show.

   C He knew why Chris blamed hypnosis for his problems.

   D He saw no link between hypnosis and schizophrenia.

4. **With which of the following statements would Paul McKenna most likely agree?**

   F Hypnosis can be very dangerous.

   G Chris' mental illness was set off by the stage hypnosis.

   H A hypnosis show is a fun and safe way to spend an evening.

   J Hypnosis can make a well person sick and a sick person well.

SUMMARIZE For each blank, choose the word that best completes the meaning of the paragraph.

schizophrenia	hypnotist	case
cause	psychiatric	theatre

For his birthday, Chris Gates' girlfriend took him to a

_____ to see a famous

_____. Nine days after the show,

Gates was admitted to a _____

hospital, where he was diagnosed with

_____. Gates later sued

the hypnotist, saying that the show was the

_____ of his illness. Gates

did not win his _____.

IF YOU WERE THERE What would you do if someone you cared about became very ill after seeing a hypnotist? Write a brief paragraph explaining your actions. Be sure to include examples from the story to support your response.

_____

_____

_____

_____

_____

_____

Who Killed Kristine Fitzhugh?

When Kristine Fitzhugh was murdered in her home, friends and neighbors were shocked. When her husband Kenneth was arrested as the killer, people were downright flabbergasted.

The Fitzhughs had been married for 33 years. They seemed like the perfect couple. Fifty-three-year-old Kristine was a music teacher in Palo Alto, California. Kenneth, 56, was a businessman. The Fitzhughs lived in a beautiful $2 million home. They spent their free time hosting parties, jogging, and playing with their two dogs.

Then, on May 5, 2000, Kristine's bloody body was found lying at the bottom of her basement stairs. Kenneth and two family friends discovered the body. At first, most people assumed it was a terrible accident. It looked like Kristine had slipped and hit her head while walking down the stairs.

But the truth was much more gruesome. Kristine had been beaten and strangled to death. Police determined that she had been killed in the kitchen. The killer had moved her body to the basement to make it look like an accident.

Police detectives quickly turned their attention to Kenneth Fitzhugh. He said he had been out near a local golf course when the murder occurred. But no one could verify his story. In addition, police found some suspicious things in his car. They found a pair of Kenneth's running shoes with blood on the soles. They found a crumpled paper towel with blood on it. And they found a bloody shirt that belonged to Kenneth. The blood on all these items came from Kristine.

At first, Kenneth said he didn't know why there was blood on his shoes. Then he began saying that Kristine had cut her finger a week before her death. When he helped her bandage it, some of her blood dripped onto his shoes. As for the shirt and paper towel, he said he had wiped his hands on these things after trying to revive Kristine.

Still, Kenneth couldn't explain how the bloody items got into his car. The police concluded that Kenneth had killed Kristine and then hidden the evidence in the car. On May 19, 2000, they arrested Kenneth for the murder of his wife.

The case came to trial in the summer of 2001. By then, Kenneth had taken an unusual step. He had asked to be hypnotized. Hypnosis is a state of deep relaxation. When people are hypnotized, they are sometimes able to open their subconscious mind. That lets them remember things they thought they had forgotten. Kenneth hoped hypnosis would help him remember how the bloody items got into his car.

According to Kenneth and his lawyers, it worked. Kenneth told the court that his hypnosis session was "a lot like looking at a movie." It enabled him to recall many new details about the day of the murder. He now remembered sitting at the kitchen table after trying to revive Kristine. As he sat there, he said, it had occurred to him that the couple's two dogs, Boots and Raina, were in his car. He thought he should go check on them. So he got up and headed outside. He was still carrying the old shirt and the paper towel he had used to wipe blood from his hands.

At the front door, he saw his running shoes. Thinking that he would need these when he took the dogs for a walk, he picked the shoes up and brought them along. Kenneth admitted that he wasn't thinking straight. He was reeling from the horrible events of the day.

Upon reaching the car, Kenneth had opened the door. "As I'm climbing in, the little dog grabs the paper towel," he said. Kenneth didn't bother to retrieve the paper towel. Instead, "I put the [shirt] under the driver's seat, put the shoes on the floor of the car, patted Boots on the head and walked back to the house." He said he left the shirt in the car because he knew it was bloody and he didn't want it to get mixed back in with regular things in the house.

Prosecutor Michael Fletcher did not believe Kenneth's story for a minute. Fletcher asked Kenneth's hypnotist if people can lie under hypnosis. "People lie in hypnosis, they lie out of hypnosis," the hypnotist admitted.

Psychologist Lisa Butler agreed. Hypnosis, she said, is "not some special pathway to the truth." Butler said that hypnosis can help bring memories to the surface. But there is no guarantee those memories are accurate. "Hypnosis is no better or worse than regular memory," she said.

Prosecutors then questioned other people who had been at the Fitzhugh house that day. One person remembered Kenneth checking on the dogs. But according to this person, the only thing Kenneth was carrying was his car keys.

In the end, jurors did not believe Kenneth's story. They found him guilty of Kristine's murder. They were convinced that he was the one who had so brutally ended her life.

If you have been timed while reading this article, enter your reading time below. Then turn to the Words-per-Minute Table on page 120 and look up your reading speed (words per minute). Enter your reading speed on the graph on page 121.

Reading Time: Selection 2

_____ : _____
MINUTES   SECONDS

UNDERSTANDING IDEAS Circle the letter of the best answer.

1. **One reason that friends of the Fitzhughs were so shocked when Kenneth was arrested for his wife's murder was because**

   A it was Kristine who had the violent temper

   B the couple had been married for 33 years

   C the couple lived in a $2 million home

   D Kristine had been known to fall down the stairs

2. **What did all the evidence found in Kenneth's car have in common?**

   F The evidence was found under the back seat.

   G All the things in the car belonged to Kristine.

   H Each piece of evidence could have been the murder weapon.

   J Kristine's blood was on everything.

3. **Kenneth's request to be hypnotized may have been an indication of his**

   A innocence

   B poor health

   C stupidity

   D blameworthiness

4. **Kenneth's own hypnotist probably helped convict Kenneth when he said that**

   F people can still lie under hypnosis

   G Kenneth was under hypnosis when he killed his wife

   H Kenneth had been diagnosed with a mental illness prior to May 5, 2000

   J people who are hypnotized can still choose between right and wrong

SUMMARIZE For each blank, choose the word that best completes the meaning of the paragraph.

truth	guilty	brutally	
alibi	evidence	jury	hypnosis

Kenneth Fitzhugh's _____

just wasn't good enough. He said he was on the golf

course when his wife was _____

murdered in their home. But there was no one who

could vouch for the fact that Kenneth was telling

the _____. Add the

_____ found in his car, and

Kenneth looked _____.

Under _____ Kenneth said that

he did not kill his wife, but it didn't convince the

_____.

IF YOU WERE THERE Imagine that you are on the jury hearing Kenneth's case. What do you believe really happened on May 5, 2000? Write a brief paragraph explaining whether you would vote "guilty" or "not guilty." Be sure to include examples from the story to support your response.

_____

_____

_____

_____

_____

USE CONTEXT CLUES When you read, you may find a word whose meaning is unfamiliar to you. When that happens, you can look up the word's meaning in the dictionary. You can also find out what the word means by looking for context clues. These are words or sentences that come before or after the word. Context clues can be words with the same or opposite meanings as the unfamiliar word. They may also be an example or definition of the unfamiliar word.

Read each excerpt from the stories you just read. Circle the letter with the best meaning of the underlined word.

1. So when McKenna asked for volunteers, Chris didn't really have a choice. "It was just a compulsion," said Chris, "and I shot out of my chair and went up on stage."
   A fit of insanity
   B bad judgment
   C free choice
   D uncontrollable force

2. McKenna said he watched for signs of distress in his volunteers. If any of them seemed upset, he offered them the chance to stop.
   F falling asleep
   G temper
   H emotional trouble
   J deceit

3. But the judge saw no link between hypnosis and schizophrenia. It was just a coincidence that Chris' illness appeared so soon after McKenna's show.
   A a habit
   B a mental disease
   C a preplanned event
   D a cause of hypnosis

4. But the truth was much more gruesome. Kristine had been beaten and strangled to death.
   F calm
   G hideous
   H tricky
   J quick

5. He said he had been out near a local golf course when the murder occurred. But no one could verify his story.
   A confirm
   B rewrite
   C choose
   D falsify

PUT WORDS INTO CONTEXT Complete the paragraph using the underlined words from the exercise on this page.

Chris Gates said that it was a

_____ that got him up on stage at Paul McKenna's show. Gates believed it was no coincidence that he became mentally ill with

_____ after participating. In another bizarre case, Kenneth Fitzhugh maintained that he was

not responsible for the _____

murder of his wife Kristine. However, because no one

could _____ his testimony, he was

found guilty of the crime.

ROOTS IN NUMBER WORDS As you have learned, one way of finding out the meaning of a word is by looking for its root. If you know the meaning of a root word, you can often decipher the meaning of a word you don't know. Many of the number words we use in English have Latin and Greek roots. The chart below shows some examples.

meaning	Greek	Latin	examples
one or single	mono	uni	unified, monopolize
two or pair	di	bi, duo	bicycle, duo
three	tri	tri	triad, triangle
ten	dec, deca, deka	deci	decade, decimal
thousands	khilo (kilo)	milli	million, kilometer

Read both complete paragraphs. For each numbered blank, refer to the word choices at the bottom of the right column. Choose a word that best completes the meaning of the story.

Less than a (1) _____ ago, a

man named Chris Gates sued Paul McKenna, claiming

that his schizophrenia had been caused by hypnosis.

While Gates was hypnotized, he actually believed he had

won a (2) _____ dollars. After the

show, Gates' boss and girlfriend noticed changes in his

personality. Gates and his therapist were (3)

_____ in their view that McKenna

was to blame.

In the last two years, there was a sad story about

Kenneth and Kristine Fitzhugh. The Fitzhughs had been

married 33 years, and the (4) _____

liked to spend their time hosting parties and jogging.

All seemed well until Kristine's body was found at

the bottom of the stairs in the couple's home.

According to prosecutors, Kenneth left a (5)

_____ of evidence in his car

that was eventually enough to convict him.

Perhaps the jury believed that Kenneth wanted to (6)

_____ the couple's money. Friends

of the Fitzhughs never expected Kristine to be murdered,

much less Kenneth arrested and accused of the crime.

1. **A** decimal
   B bicycle
   C triangle
   D decade

2. **F** million
   G decimal
   H kilometer
   J triangle

3. **A** three
   B unified
   C single
   D bicycle

4. **F** duo
   G ten
   H thousands
   J three

5. **A** one
   B triad
   C unified
   D decimal

6. **F** pair
   G single
   H monopolize
   J bicycle

FIND THE PURPOSE You already know that authors write to inform or teach, to persuade or convince, or to entertain. You also know that many times authors write for more than one purpose. Advertisements, for example, can fit all three purposes for writing. The ad may inform you about a product or service you can buy. It attempts to persuade you to buy it, and often, ads are entertaining so that they appeal readily to a large number of people.

Review the chart below. Then choose the best answer to each question.

AUTHOR'S PURPOSE		
to inform (teach)	**to persuade (convince)**	**to entertain (amuse)**
• textbook	• editorials	• fictional stories
• newspaper and magazine articles	• advertisements	• poems
• nonfiction stories/books	• position papers (for or against an issue)	• humorous essays, books, or cartoons
• reviews (movies, books, music, and so on)	• lawyer's briefs (arguments)	• anecdotes (personal stories)

1. **"Is Hypnosis Dangerous?" is an example of a passage that should appear under which heading?**

   A to inform

   B to persuade

   C to entertain

   D all of the above

2. **If "Who Killed Kristine Fitzhugh?" was an article in the editorial page of your newspaper, which heading would it be likely to appear under on the chart?**

   F to inform

   G to persuade

   H to entertain

   J all of the above

3. **If Chris Gates' therapist, Derek Crussell, wrote a paper about Gates' case for the courtroom, under which heading would it appear?**

   A to inform

   B to persuade

   C to entertain

   D all of the above

4. **If the president of the Safe Hypnosis Association wrote a letter to the editor of the local paper in support of Paul McKenna, under which heading on the chart would that letter appear?**

   F to inform

   G to persuade

   H to entertain

   J all of the above

WRITE WITH A PURPOSE Write a topic sentence about the different aspects of hypnosis for each of the purposes you reviewed in this lesson.

to inform: _____

_____

to persuade: _____

_____

to entertain: _____

_____

VERIFYING EVIDENCE Because a lot of misinformation gets printed, you must verify the accuracy of everything you read. The way to do that is to weigh the evidence presented and decide whether it is trustworthy. Sometimes part of an article may present the correct facts about something, and part of the article may deliberately mislead you. You have to decide whether to believe all or only parts of it. Read the following imaginary testimony from hypnotist Paul McKenna and then choose the best answer for each question.

[1] I've been doing these shows for years. [2] People love to come up on stage and be hypnotized in front of their friends. [3] I'm always very careful, and my hypnosis is entirely safe. [4] No one's personality changes as a result of being hypnotized. [5] I don't have that kind of power. [6] Hypnosis is nothing more than a deep relaxation technique. [7] Medical experts have said that it is impossible to use hypnosis to make someone sick who is normally well. [8] I feel sorry for Mr. Gates, but I am not responsible for his illness.

1. **What evidence is missing from the paragraph?**
   A whether McKenna thinks he is innocent
   B how sick Chris Gates is
   C the names of the experts that McKenna quotes
   D how experienced McKenna is

2. **Which of the following sentences would be most important to verify?**
   F Sentence 1
   G Sentence 2
   H Sentence 4
   J Sentence 8

JUDGE THE EVIDENCE To persuade the reader of an opinion or story, the author often provides evidence. It is up to the reader to judge if the evidence presented is believable or not.

1. **Which of the following would be the most convincing in a courtroom?**
   A case histories
   B an eyewitness account
   C a doctor's opinion
   D testimony of the accused person

2. **Which statement best supports Chris Gates' story from "Is Hypnosis Dangerous?"**
   F Chris was exceptionally entertaining during the hypnosis.
   G Paul McKenna was found innocent of wrongdoing.
   H Chris Gates felt like he had been hypnotized while he was still in his chair.
   J Chris Gates had no history of mental illness.

PERSUADE WITH EVIDENCE Write two sentences persuading your reader that hypnosis is either dangerous or not dangerous. Be sure to include examples from the stories to support your answer.

_____

_____

_____

_____

_____

_____

Nostradamus

Michel de Nostradame seemed like an ordinary child. There was nothing about his early years to suggest that he had any special powers. He grew up in a wealthy French family in the 1500s. As a young man he studied medicine. He became a doctor in the south of France. But while his early life seemed ordinary, his later years were quite extraordinary. In his 40s, he began making predictions about the future. By the end of his life, "Nostradamus" had become one of the world's greatest prophets.

In 1555, Nostradamus wanted to publish some of his predictions. But he knew he had to be careful. His words might get him in trouble. After all, this was the age of the Inquisition. Leaders of the Catholic Church were arresting anyone who disagreed with them. Inquisition leaders were already suspicious of Nostradamus. If he issued prophecies they disliked, they might arrest him.

And so Nostradamus protected himself. He published his prophecies, but he deliberately made them hard to understand. He wrote his book as a series of four-line poems called "quatrains." Each one offered a look into the future. But readers had to study the words carefully to figure out what they meant. In the preface to *Centuries*, Nostradamus admitted that the book

was written in an "obscure" style. Still, he believed that a "reasoning and intelligent being" should be able to understand it.

Nostradamus' book intrigued many people. Even the Queen of France was interested. Perhaps that was because one prophecy seemed to involve her husband, King Henry II. In Quatrain #1-35, Nostradamus wrote:

> "The young lion will overcome
>   the older one,
>   in a field of combat in a single fight.
>   He will pierce his eyes in
>   their golden cage;
>   two wounds in one, then he dies
>   a cruel death."

Since Henry II used the lion as his symbol, it seemed logical that he was the "older" lion. But who was the young one? What sort of battle would involve just a single fight? Men wore helmets during battle, so how could an opponent pierce Henry's eyes?

The prediction seemed far-fetched at best. And yet, four years later, everything in that quatrain came true. In July 1559, Henry held a jousting contest. The king competed against a younger man—the Comte de Montgomery. Both men had lions on their shields. During the contest, Montgomery's lance hit Henry's gold helmet. A splinter from the lance shot through the hole in Henry's visor. It passed through the king's eye and lodged in his brain. Henry suffered terribly for ten days. Then he died.

Everyone was stunned. How could Nostradamus have known? Some people were upset with him. But others looked at him with new respect. More and more important figures came to see him. And more people began reading his book.

Nostradamus died in 1566. But his prophecies lived on. He had always said that some would not come to pass for many years. In fact, some might not come true for centuries. Over the years, different quatrains have seemed to fit important events. One seems to point toward the French Revolution. Several seem connected to World War II. After terrorists attacked America on September 11, 2001, people checked to see if Nostradamus had predicted *that*. Some thought he had. Quatrain #10-72 includes these words:

"... from the sky will come the Great King of Terror ..."

To some, that was a clear reference to Osama Bin Laden, the man behind the attack. Once again, the name Nostradamus was in the news.

But a closer look raised doubts about how special Nostradamus' powers really were. For one thing, most quatrains contain a lot of gibberish. There may be just a few words that fit an event. Consider the rest of Quatrain #10-72:

"In the year 1999, in the seventh month,
from the sky will come the Great King of Terror,
bringing back to life the great king of the Mongols.

Before and after, Mars to reign by good fortune."

The terrorist attack did not take place in the seventh month of 1999. Osama Bin Laden is not a Mongol. And it's hard to know *what* the last line means.

In fact, it is hard to figure out most of Nostradamus' prophecies. They are so vague that they could be applied to hundreds of situations. Even the prophecy about the "young lion" could be interpreted a number of ways. And consider Quatrain #6-97:

"Five and forty steps the sky will burn
Fire approaching the large new city
Instantly a great thin flame will leap
When someone will want to test the Normans."

As one critic points out, it doesn't take much insight to guess that a fire will break out in a large city sometime over the next several hundred years. Some say it predicts the Great Chicago Fire of 1871. Others say it predicts the September 11 attack. And others say it is like all of Nostradamus' other prophecies: pure nonsense.

If you have been timed while reading this article, enter your reading time below. Then turn to the Words-per-Minute Table on page 120 and look up your reading speed (words per minute). Enter your reading speed on the graph on page 121.

Reading Time: Selection 1

_____ : _____
MINUTES   SECONDS

UNDERSTANDING IDEAS Circle the letter of the best answer.

1. **Which statement best compares Nostradamus' early life with his later life?**

   A He grew up in a wealthy French family in the 1500s.

   B As a young man he studied medicine and later became a doctor.

   C When he reached age 40, he started making predictions about the future.

   D His early life seemed ordinary, but his later years were quite extraordinary.

2. **Why did Nostradamus deliberately make his predictions hard to understand?**

   F Church leaders might arrest him.

   G He wrote them as four-line poems.

   H Readers had to study the words carefully

   J He wanted "reasoning and intelligent" readers.

3. **Which statement is true about Nostradamus' predictions?**

   A They have helped people avoid dangerous situations.

   B They are all far-fetched and they never really come true.

   C They are so vague that they could be applied to hundreds of situations.

   D They are written in an obscure style, but anyone can understand them.

4. **Those who believe that Nostradamus predicted the September 11, 2001, tragedy are most likely people who**

   F think anyone can guess that something from the sky can cause a disaster

   G connect every major event or disaster to one of Nostradamus' predictions

   H have serious doubts about how special Nostradamus' powers really were

   J think that his quartrains can mean anything that people want them to mean

SUMMARIZE For each blank, choose the word that best completes the meaning of the paragraph.

| arrested | ordinary | predicted |
| quatrains | believe | prophets |

Nostradamus grew up like any

_____ child, but he became one

of the world's greatest _____.

Afraid of being _____,

he deliberately published vague four-line poems called

_____. One of his poems

_____ how King Henry II

would die and it did happen. Some people

_____ that Nostradamus has

predicted every major event in the world including

September 11, 2001.

IF YOU WERE THERE If you knew Nostradamus, what question would you ask him? Write your question and then write a brief answer from Nostradamus. Be sure to include examples from the story to support your response.

_____
_____
_____
_____
_____

The Wreck of the Titanic

"She was the largest craft afloat and the greatest of the works of men." This was the opening line of a book written by Morgan Robertson. The book, titled *Futility*, told the story of a huge ocean liner. When the ship was built, everyone believed it was unsinkable. But on a trip across the Atlantic, it hit an iceberg and sank. Most of the people on board drowned. Robertson wrote his book in 1898. At the time, it seemed like a wild piece of fiction. But fourteen years later a huge ship really did sink in the Atlantic. After the *Titanic* went down, people took another look at Robertson's book. They couldn't believe it. Dozens of details from the book matched the actual event. It seemed that Morgan Robertson had foretold the future.

To begin with, there was the name of the ships. Robertson called his ship the *Titan*. That was very close to the real-life *Titanic*. Both Robertson's ship and the *Titanic* were British. Both were sailing between England and New York.

Then there was the size of the vessels. When Robertson wrote his book, he imagined a ship far bigger than current technology could support. By the time the real *Titanic* was built, technology had improved. Robertson's imaginings had come true. In fact,

Robertson guessed the size and power of the *Titanic* almost exactly. Robertson's ship weighed forty-five thousand tons. The *Titanic* weighed about forty-six thousand tons. Robertson's ship was 800 feet long. The *Titanic* was 882 feet. Each ship could travel at a top speed of 24 knots. Each used three propellers. And each could carry about 3,000 people.

The similarity between the ships was spooky enough. But it was as though Robertson had looked into the future and seen the *Titanic's* fate. Robertson envisioned a scene in the North Atlantic. He writes of a dark April night. A huge "unsinkable" ship cuts through the icy water at full speed. Suddenly, around midnight, the ship hits an iceberg. The collision rips open the watertight compartments that keep the ship afloat.

Fourteen years later, this is exactly what happened to the *Titanic*. How could Robertson have known that such an accident would take place? And how could he have known that it would occur about a hundred miles south of Greenland? Robertson got the month right. He was right about the time of night and the speed of the ship. He correctly imagined that the iceberg would hit the forward starboard side. He even described how the ship's stern would tilt high into the air just before the vessel sank.

In Robertson's book, there are about two thousand passengers on board. Yet there are only 24 lifeboats. No one thinks this is a problem because no one thinks lifeboats will ever be needed. And so it was with the *Titanic*. The *Titanic* set sail with about 2,200 passengers. No one cared that there were only 20 lifeboats. No one thought the *Titanic* would ever sink. On the *Titanic,* as on Robertson's *Titan,* people put their faith in modern technology. They believed their manmade ship was stronger than any force of nature. In both cases, this was a tragic mistake. The resulting loss of life was staggering.

After the *Titanic* sank, people took a new interest in Robertson's book. Two different magazines reprinted it. Later it was printed again, with the title *The Wreck of the Titan.* People combed through the pages trying to find all the matches between the book and the real disaster. By some counts, there were more than fifty.

Were these matches just coincidences? Or was it possible that Robertson somehow knew what the future held? Robertson himself claimed that he had tapped into some strange psychic power. He told one woman that he had an "astral writing partner." This partner helped him move into a world where "there is no such thing as Time."

To some people, this seemed like a good explanation. Surely it didn't make sense to think that Robertson had just made a lot of lucky guesses. In fact, some people calculated the likelihood of him getting so many things right. They put the odds at four billion to one.

Others think the odds were better than that. They say the chances were closer to a thousand to one. Still, Robertson would have needed an amazing streak of luck to get so many details right. Given that, some have concluded that Morgan Robertson really did have extraordinary vision. They believe he somehow reached across time and space to see the future.

He only foresaw one event. But it was one that shook the world.

If you have been timed while reading this article, enter your reading time below. Then turn to the Words-per-Minute Table on page 120 and look up your reading speed (words per minute). Enter your reading speed on the graph on page 121.

Reading Time: Selection 2

_____ : _____
MINUTES   SECONDS

UNDERSTANDING IDEAS Circle the letter of the best answer.

1. What future event did Morgan Robertson foretell?

A writing the book entitled *Futility*

B the sinking of a huge ocean liner

C the building of an unsinkable ship

D matching his book with the real disaster

2. Which statement belongs in the empty box?

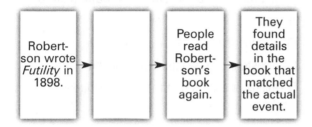

| Robert-son wrote *Futility* in 1898. | | People read Robert-son's book again. | They found details in the book that matched the actual event. |

F The *Titanic* sank in the Atlantic.

G Robertson called his ship the *Titan*.

H The *Titan* hit an iceberg and sank.

J People couldn't believe Robertson's book.

3. How did Robertson explain why his book matched the real event so closely?

A He had made a lot of lucky guesses.

B He knew that icebergs hit ships in April.

C He had tapped into some kind of psychic power.

D He knew that technology would make the *Titanic* possible.

4. Why did some people conclude that Robertson really did have extraordinary vision?

F His writing partner helped him move to a timeless world.

G He was very lucky to have guessed exactly what would happen.

H The odds of getting so many details right are four billion to one.

J Reaching across time and space to see the future is quite common.

SUMMARIZE For each blank, choose the word that best completes the meaning of the paragraph.

foresee	described	
		similar
unsinkable	vision	

In 1898 Morgan Robertson wrote about the sinking of

a ship that everyone believed was

_____. Fourteen years later

a very _____ ship called *Titanic*

really did sink in the Atlantic. It happened almost exactly

the same way as Robertson _____

the event. Robertson was able to

_____ the disaster in amazing

detail. Many people believed that he must have

possessed an extraordinary _____.

IF YOU WERE THERE Imagine that you had predicted an event that really happened. Write a brief paragraph explaining how you were able to make the prediction. Be sure to include examples from the story to support your response.

_____

_____

_____

_____

_____

USE CONTEXT CLUES When you read, you may find a word whose meaning is unfamiliar to you. When that happens, you can look up the word's meaning in the dictionary. You can also find out what the word means by looking for context clues. These are words or sentences that come before or after the word. Context clues can be words with the same or opposite meanings as the unfamiliar word. They may also be an example or definition of the unfamiliar word.

Read each excerpt from the stories you just read. Circle the letter with the best meaning of the underlined word.

1. **But while his early life seemed ordinary, his later years were quite <u>extraordinary</u>. In his 40s, he began making predictions about the future.**

   A amazing

   B common

   C everyday

   D large

2. **In his 40s, he began making predictions about the future. By the end of his life, "Nostradamus" had become one of the world's greatest <u>prophets</u>.**

   F poets who write quatrains

   G doctors who treat sick people

   H young people who become heroes

   J people who foretell coming events

3. **As one critic points out, it doesn't take much <u>insight</u> to guess that a fire will break out in a large city over the next several hundred years.**

   A a person's eyes

   B having a good eyesight

   C the power of seeing into a situation

   D being inside when an event happens

4. **But it was as though Robertson had looked into the future and seen the *Titanic's* fate. Robertson <u>envisioned</u> a scene in the North Atlantic.**

   F painted a picture in his mind

   G actually saw an event happen

   H entered a world in the future

   J wrote a very detailed story

5. **People combed through the pages trying to find all the matches between the book and the real disaster. By some counts there were more than fifty. Were these matches just <u>coincidences</u>?**

   A connections to a real event

   B sayings that people believe in

   C disasters that cannot really happen

   D things or events that match by accident

PUT WORDS INTO CONTEXT Complete the paragraph using the underlined words from the exercise on this page.

Is it really possible for _____

to predict the future? Their critics believe that when

predictions come true, these are mere

_____. They say that anyone with

good _____ can predict what will

happen based on current trends. But when people hear of

predictions that came true, they can't help but believe

that prophets have _____ powers.

WORDS THAT COMPARE AND CONTRAST One type of context clue likens or contrasts an unfamiliar word to a familiar word or concept. When you see words and phrases such as *alike, different, both, also, in contrast, but,* and *yet,* you can tell that a comparison or contrast of an unfamiliar term will follow.

Read the complete paragraph. For each numbered blank, refer to the word choices at the right. Choose the word that best completes the meaning of the paragraph.

Nostradamus and Morgan Robertson are

(1)_____ because of their ability to

predict future events. (2)_____,

the way they foretold events was quite

(3)_____. Nostradamus

wrote vague poems, (4)_____

Robertson wrote detailed descriptions of an event.

Robertson predicted only one event in great detail;

(5)_____, Nostradamus seemed to

have predicted several world events. Their critics believe

that (6)_____ prophets simply had

extraordinary insights into situations. Some critics even

think that (7)_____ most

prophecies, their predictions are "pure nonsense." Do you

agree or (8)_____ with the critics?

1. A also
   B same
   C too
   D alike

2. F Similarly
   G Likewise
   H However
   J Though

3. A another
   B different
   C separate
   D unlike

4. F while
   G similarly
   H on one hand
   J in other ways

5. A and
   B in contrast
   C although
   D in other ways

6. F like
   G same
   H both
   J equal

7. A like
   B comparable
   C similar
   D matching

8. F disagree
   G unlike
   H contrast
   J distint

ORGANIZE THE FACTS To understand a passage, you should ask questions about the text before, during, and after reading and then look for answers. While you are reading, know how and where to look for answers to questions. Sometimes the answer might be stated directly in the passage; other times you need to put ideas or information together to come up with the answer. Then sometimes the answer may not be in the passage at all, but may be something you already know.

Use the information in the chart below to choose the best answer to each question in the next column.

Question-Answer Relationships	
Question	**How to Answer**
• Who predicted the death of Henry II?	Question words such as *who, where,* and *when* usually indicate that the answer is right there in the passage.
• What caused people to think that Nostradamus predicted September 11?	The question words *what* and *why* sometimes require you to think and to search the passage.
• Why are prophets extraordinary?	A general question like this is about something you probably know. You can come up with the answer on your own.
• How do you think people would act if Robertson wrote a book about a plane crash?	A question that asks what you think requires you to use what you already know and what the author tells you. You will make an inference or draw a conclusion.

1. **Which question can you answer by looking for a direct statement from the story?**
   A Where did Nostradamus grow up?
   B Why was he called a prophet?
   C How did readers figure out his predictions?
   D What caused church leaders to arrest prophets?

2. **Which question can you answer by thinking and searching?**
   F Where did the *Titanic* sink?
   G When did Robertson write his book?
   H What was the book *Futility* about?
   J How do you think Robertson foretold the future?

3. **Which question requires you to use what you already know from experience and what the author tells you?**
   A Where did the *Titanic* sink?
   B Why were people stunned when Henry II died?
   C What caused the *Titan* to sink?
   D How do you think Robertson's critics explain the match between the *Titan* and the *Titanic*?

WRITE YOUR OWN QUESTIONS Write two questions about each of the stories in this unit. For each question, explain how you would find the answer.

_____

_____

_____

_____

_____

_____

MAKE PREDICTIONS You can make predictions, or educated guesses, based on what you already know. For example, you already know that some people believe Nostradamus predicted disasters such as what happened on September 11, 2001. Based on this knowledge, you can reasonably predict that if another major disaster happens, they will connect the event with one of Nostradamus' poems.

Read this passage, and answer the following questions based on what you know after reading the stories.

[1] Everyday Prophets, a new organization for people who want to study prophecies, is inviting new members to join. [2] Mrs. Mila Simpson, the organization's expert on Nostradamus, claims that her group can train people to develop their powers of prediction. [3] She says the only requirement is that a person should have good insights. [4] The organization offers courses that compare prophecies with actual events.

1. **What would a person who believes in Nostradamus most likely do next?**

   A foretell the future

   B become a prophet

   C join the organization

   D report on Nostradamus

2. **Which sentence in the passage helps you predict that a person who joins will most likely study comparisons between actual events and Nostradamus' prophecies?**

   F Sentence 1

   G Sentence 2

   H Sentence 3

   J Sentence 4

JUDGE THE BASIS OF A PREDICTION For predictions to be reasonably accurate, they must be based on what you know as factual information. Choose the best answer.

1. **Which statement helps you predict that skeptics will brush aside another prophecy by Nostradamus?**

   A Anyone could become a prophet if he or she studies hard.

   B Nostradamus' poems may be vague, but they contain a lot of truth.

   C It takes tremendous powers to be able to predict what will happen in the future.

   D They believe that all of Nostradamus' prophecies are pure nonsense.

2. **Which statement helps you predict that people would connect an important event to one of Nostradamus' quatrains?**

   F Although Nostradamus died in 1566, his prophecies live on.

   G Over the years, different quatrains have seemed to fit important events.

   H Nostradamus' prophecies could be interpreted in a number of ways.

   J A closer look raised doubts about how special Nostradamus' powers really were.

PREDICT WHAT YOU WOULD DO Write a brief paragraph explaining what you would do if a friend tells you about a Nostradamus prophecy that is about to happen. Use examples from the stories you just read to explain your predictions.

_____

_____

_____

_____

_____

Words-per-Minute Table

If you were timed while reading, find your reading time in the column on the left. Find the unit and number of the story across the top of the chart. Follow the time row across to its intersection with the column of the story. This is your reading speed. Go to the next page to plot your progress.

Unit	1		2		3		4		5		6		7		8		9		10	
Selection \ Time	1	2	1	2	1	2	1	2	1	2	1	2	1	2	1	2	1	2	1	2
1:20	917	861	901	854	826	770	838	773	891	838	934	910	891	902	884	892	877	935	827	773
1:40	688	646	676	641	620	578	629	580	668	629	701	683	668	679	663	669	658	617	641	580
2:00	550	516	540	512	496	462	503	464	534	503	560	546	534	540	530	535	526	494	512	464
2:20	459	431	386	427	413	385	419	387	446	419	467	455	446	386	442	446	439	412	427	387
2:40	393	369	338	366	354	330	359	314	382	359	400	390	382	338	379	382	376	353	366	314
3:00	344	323	338	320	310	289	229	290	334	279	350	341	334	300	331	334	329	309	320	290
3:20	306	287	300	285	275	257	251	244	297	251	311	303	297	270	295	297	292	274	285	244
3:40	275	258	270	256	248	231	229	220	267	229	280	273	267	246	265	268	263	247	256	220
4:00	250	235	246	233	225	210	210	211	243	210	255	248	243	225	241	243	239	224	233	211
4:20	229	215	225	214	207	193	190	193	223	190	234	228	223	208	221	223	219	206	214	193
4:40	212	373	208	197	191	178	180	169	206	180	216	210	206	193	204	206	202	190	197	169
5:00	197	184	193	183	177	165	180	157	191	168	200	195	191	178	189	191	188	176	183	157
5:20	183	172	180	171	165	154	168	155	178	157	187	182	178	180	177	178	175	165	171	155
5:40	172	161	169	160	155	144	157	145	167	148	175	171	167	169	166	167	164	154	160	145
6:00	162	152	159	151	146	136	148	136	157	140	165	161	157	159	156	157	155	145	151	136
6:20	153	143	150	142	138	128	140	129	149	132	156	152	149	150	147	149	146	137	142	129
6:40	145	136	142	135	130	122	132	122	141	126	148	144	141	142	140	141	138	130	135	122
7:00	138	129	135	128	124	116	126	116	134	120	140	136	134	135	133	134	132	123	128	116
7:20	131	123	129	122	118	110	120	110	127	114	133	130	127	129	126	127	125	118	122	110
7:40	125	117	123	116	113	105	114	105	122	109	127	124	122	123	121	122	120	112	116	105
8:00	120	112	118	111	108	100	109	101	116	105	122	119	116	118	115	116	114	107	111	101
8:20	115	108	113	107	103	96	105	97	111	101	117	114	111	113	111	112	110	103	107	97
8:40	110	103	108	102	99	92	101	93	107	97	112	109	107	108	106	107	105	99	102	93
9:00	106	99	104	99	95	89	97	89	103	93	108	105	103	104	102	103	101	95	99	89
9:20	102	96	100	95	92	86	93	81	99	90	104	101	99	100	98	99	97	91	95	81
9:40	98	92	97	92	89	83	90	83	95	87	100	98	95	97	95	98	94	88	92	83
10:00	95	89	93	88	85	80	87	80	92	84	97	94	92	93	91	92	91	85	88	80
10:20	92	86	90	85	83	77	84	77	89	81	93	91	89	90	88	89	88	82	85	77
10:40	89	83	87	83	80	75	81	75	86	79	90	88	86	87	86	88	85	80	83	75
11:00	86	81	84	80	77	72	79	72	84	76	88	85	84	84	83	84	82	77	80	72
11:20	83	78	82	78	75	70	76	70	81	74	85	82	81	82	80	81	80	75	78	70
11:40	81	76	80	75	73	68	74	68	79	72	82	80	79	80	78	79	77	73	75	68
12:00	79	74	77	73	71	66	72	66	76	70	80	78	76	77	76	76	75	71	73	66
12:20	76	72	75	71	69	64	70	64	74	68	79	76	74	75	74	74	73	69	71	64
12:40	74	70	73	69	67	62	68	63	72	66	76	74	72	73	72	72	71	67	69	63
13:00	72	68	71	67	65	61	66	61	70	64	74	72	70	71	70	70	69	65	67	61
13:20	71	66	69	66	64	59	64	59	69	63	72	70	69	69	68	69	67	63	66	59
13:40	69	65	68	64	62	58	63	58	67	61	70	68	67	68	66	67	66	62	64	58
14:00	67	63	66	62	60	56	61	57	65	60	68	67	65	66	65	65	64	60	63	57
14:20	66	62	64	61	59	55	60	55	64	58	67	65	64	64	63	64	63	59	61	55
14:40	64	60	63	60	58	54	58	54	62	57	65	64	62	63	62	62	61	57	60	54
15:00	63	59	61	58	56	53	57	53	61	56	64	62	61	61	60	61	60	55	58	53

Plotting Your Progress: Reading Speed

Enter your words-per-minute rate in the box above the appropriate lesson. Then place a small X on the line directly above the number of the lesson, across from the number of words per minute you read. Graph your progress by drawing a line to connect the X's.

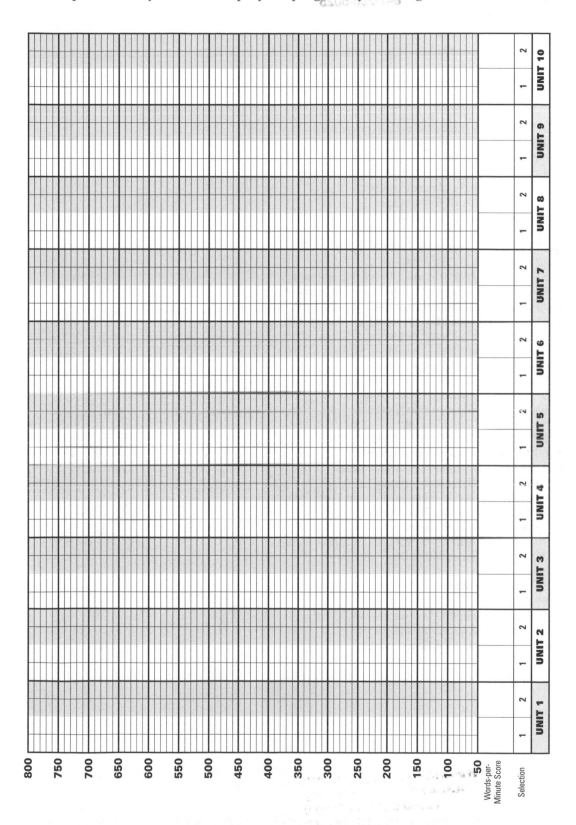

Words-per-Minute Score																				
Selection	1	2	1	2	1	2	1	2	1	2	1	2	1	2	1	2	1	2	1	2
	UNIT 1		UNIT 2		UNIT 3		UNIT 4		UNIT 5		UNIT 6		UNIT 7		UNIT 8		UNIT 9		UNIT 10	

800 750 700 650 600 550 500 450 400 350 300 250 200 150 100 50

Photo Credits

Unit 1: p. vi Table Mesa Productions Ltd./ImageState
Unit 1: p. 3 picture 1: Gettyimages
Unit 1: p. 3 picture 2: Morton Beebe, S.F./Corbis
Unit 1: p. 3 picture 3: Roger Smith/Index Stock Imagery
Unit 1: p. 3 picture 4: Perry Mastrovito/Corbis
Unit 1: p. 4 Dante Burn-Forti/Gettyimages
Unit 2: p. 12 Richard Price/Gettyimages
Unit 2: p. 16 Photovault
Unit 3: p. 24 Linda Mooney/Index Stock Imagery
Unit 3: p. 28 Peter Denton/Gettyimages
Unit 3: p. 31 picture F: Rick Friedman/Index Stock Imagery
Unit 3: p. 31 picture G: Image Network/Index Stock Imagery
Unit 3: p. 31 picture H: Chad Ehlers/Index Stock Imagery
Unit 3: p. 31 picture J: David Davis/Index Stock Imagery
Unit 4: p. 36 Keith Brofsky/Gettyimages
Unit 4: p. 40 Tony Latham/Gettyimages
Unit 5: p. 48 Tony Hopewell/Gettyimages
Unit 5: p. 52 Miguel S. Salmeron/Gettyimages
Unit 5: p. 55 picture A: Royalty Free/Corbis
Unit 5: p. 55 picture B: Royalty Free/Corbis
Unit 5: p. 55 picture C: Gettyimages
Unit 5: p. 55 picture D: Royalty Free/Corbis
Unit 6: p. 60 Jerry Kobalenko/Gettyimages
Unit 6: p. 64 Diana Duncan Holmes/Gettyimages
Unit 7: p. 72 Walter Bibikow/Gettyimages
Unit 7: p. 75 picture 1: Jacob P. Halaska/Image Stock Imagery
Unit 7: p. 75 picture 2: Royalty Free/Corbis
Unit 7: p. 75 picture 3: Gettyimages
Unit 7: p. 75 picture 4: Michael S. Yamashita/Corbis
Unit 7: p. 76 Patricia Canova/Index Stock Imagery
Unit 8: p. 84 Photovault
Unit 8: p. 88 Alexander Walter/Gettyimages
Unit 9: p. 96 Bruce T. Brown/Gettyimages
Unit 9: p. 100 Claire Arnaud/Gettyimages
Unit 10: p. 108 Tony Latham/Gettyimages
Unit 10: p. 112 Hulton/Archive/Gettyimages